SIMPLY
DELICIOUS

ITALIAN

SIMPLY
DELICIOUS

ITALIAN

Carla Bardi

Zak
BOOKS

Simply Delicious Italian
was created and produced by McRae Books Srl
Via del Salviatino 1 – 50016 Fiesole (Florence), Italy
info@mcraebooks.com
Publishers: Anne McRae and Marco Nardi
Project Director: Anne McRae
Design: Sara Mathews
Text: Carla Bardi
Photography: Studio Marco Lanza
Home Economist: Benedetto Rillo
Artbuying: McRae Books
Layouts: Aurora Granata
Repro: Fotolito Raf, Florence
Pre-press: Filippo Delle Monache

Barnes & Noble
122 Fifth Avenue
New York, NY 10011

ISBN-13: 978-1-4351-0199-9
ISBN-10: 1-4351-0199-5

Printed and bound in China

10 9 8 7 6 5 4 3 2 1

Table of Contents

APPETIZERS

SERVES 4–6

PREPARATION 10 min

DIFFICULTY level 1

Deli Meats
with melon and fresh figs

Wipe the cantaloupe with a damp cloth and cut it in half. Slice each half into 4 to 6 wedges and arrange them on a serving dish with the prosciutto.

If liked, cut the skin off the cantaloupe using a sharp knife and place the wedges of fruit back into the skins to serve.

Rinse the figs carefully under cold running water. Pat dry with paper towels. Trim the stalks, then cut each fig into four.

Remove the rind from the salami. If using, place the fig leaves on a large serving dish and arrange the salami and figs on top.

5 oz (150 g) prosciutto, thinly sliced
1 medium cantaloupe (rock melon)
8–12 large green or black figs
5 oz (150 g) salami, thinly sliced
Fresh fig leaves, to serve (optional)

Suggested wine: a dry sparkling white
(Prosecco di Conegliano)

SERVES 4–6

PREPARATION 5 min

DIFFICULTY level 1

Mixed Deli Meats

Arrange the various meats on a serving platter or dish. Place the bread in a bread basket and serve with the meats, olives, and pickles.

Given the popularity of Italian food, all the deli meats listed here can usually be found in Italian delicatessens or the specialist sections of large supermarkets or city food stores. However, if you can't find the exact ones, replace with other, similar types of Italian deli meats. Finocchiona, for example, is a fennel-flavored salami made in Tuscany; replace it with another soft, crumbly salami.

- 5 oz (150 g) prosciutto, freshly sliced off the ham
- 4 oz (125 g) sliced salami
- 4 oz (125 g) finocchiona, sliced fairly thickly
- 6 small wild boar sausages
- 1 lb (500 g) firm-textured white bread, sliced

Best quality green or black olives

Homemade pickles (optional)

Suggested wine: a dry, fruity red (Chianti Classico)

Raw Vegetables
in olive oil dip

Only the freshest, most tender artichokes are suitable. Have one or two large, juicy lemon wedges ready to rub over all the cut surfaces as you work to prevent discoloration. Cut off the upper section of the remaining leaves, leaving the fleshy, edible base of each leaf attached to the stem. Doing this will expose a central "cone" of leaves: slice about 1 inch (2.5 cm) off the top and part the leaves to gain access to the "choke;" the spiny filaments which must be carefully trimmed away, leaving the fleshy heart intact. Use a small, sharp knife to scrape away the skin from the stalk. As each artichoke is finished, drop it into a bowl of cold water acidulated with lemon juice. Set aside for 15 minutes.

If the carrots are very young and tender, scrub well and leave whole with the tops attached. If larger, peel and cut lengthwise into quarters.

Discard the outermost layer of the fennel leaves, cut the bulbs from top to bottom, dividing them into quarters, and rinse well.

Cut the celery heart lengthwise in half or quarters, wash and drain.

Trim and wash the radishes, leaving any fresh, unwilted leaves attached.

Trim the spring onions, leaving only a short length of green leaf attached. Unless they are very fresh and firm, remove the outermost layer of the bulb.

Drain the artichokes well and pat dry with paper towels.

Arrange all the vegetables on a large serving platter. Place the platter in the middle of the table and give each person a plate and a small bowl. Place containers of oil, vinegar, freshly squeezed lemon juice, salt, and pepper on the table and let each diner prepare their own bowl of dressing to dip the vegetables into.

Serve with plenty of fresh bread.

4–6 very young, fresh globe artichokes
Lemon wedges
12 very fresh small carrots, preferably with their tops
2 small tender fennel bulbs
1 celery heart
12 radishes
6 spring onions
1/2 cup (125 ml) extra-virgin olive oil
Good quality wine vinegar
1/3 cup (90 ml) freshly squeezed lemon juice
Salt and freshly ground black pepper
Freshly baked bread, to serve

Suggested wine: a dry, sparkling white (Spumante di Vernaccia di San Gimignano)

Piquant Olives

Pit the olives and press them with the heel of your hand to crush slightly.

Place in a bowl and add all the remaining ingredients. Stir well, then leave to stand for at least 4 hours before serving to let the flavors penetrate.

These tasty olives will keep for up to a week if stored in a tightly closed container in the refrigerator.

For a slightly different but equally delicious dish, prepare the olives Sicilian-style, by adding 1 tablespoon of capers, a handful of chopped mint leaves, and a finely chopped heart of crisp green celery.

10 oz (300 g) large green olives, pickled in brine

2 cloves garlic, thinly sliced

1 small chile pepper, seeded and finely chopped

1/4 cup (60 ml) extra-virgin olive oil

1 tablespoon red wine vinegar

2 teaspoons finely chopped fresh oregano or 1 teaspoon dried oregano

Suggested wine: a dry red (Cerasuolo)

Fava Beans
with pecorino

This is a typical appetizer from Tuscany and Umbria, served in the early spring when crisp young fava beans arrive in the farmer's markets. In Tuscany, it is served with fresh pecorino—called *marzolino* (March cheese). It is just as good with any pecorino (sheep's cheese). Don't serve with pecorino romano, which is a grating cheese (great on pasta).

Rinse the beans thoroughly under cold running water. Dry well on a clean dishcloth. Discard any tough or withered-looking pods, or any with ugly spots or marks. Place in an attractive serving dish.

Serve with the cheese already cut into dice, or in a wedge freshly cut from the round forms.

4 lb (2 kg) fresh, young fava beans (broad beans) in their pods

12 oz (350 g) fresh young pecorino cheese

Suggested wine: a dry, aromatic white (Bianco Capena)

SERVES 4

PREPARATION 10 min + 20 min to drain

COOKING 5 min

DIFFICULTY level 1

Bruschette
with tomato and basil

Cut the tomatoes in half, sprinkle with salt, and set them upside-down in a colander for 20 minutes to drain.

Toast the bread until golden brown over a barbecue or in the oven (so that it dries out and is very crisp). If you toast the bread in a toaster it will be too moist and the bruschette will be soggy.

Rub the slices of toast with the garlic. Season with salt and pepper and drizzle with half the oil.

Chop the tomatoes in small cubes. Arrange them on the toast and garnish with the basil. Drizzle with the remaining oil and serve immediately.

4 medium salad tomatoes
4 large slices firm-textured bread
2 cloves garlic
Salt and freshly ground black pepper
1/3 cup (90 ml) extra-virgin olive oil
Fresh basil leaves, torn

Suggested wine: a light dry white
    (Soave Classico)

Tuna Crostini
with pickles

Place the tuna, cocktail onions, pickled vegetables (except a few to garnish) and mayonnaise in a food processor and chop until smooth.

Spread on the bread, garnish with the reserved vegetables and serve.

- 8 oz (250 g) canned tuna, drained
- 2 oz (60 g) cocktail onions
- 3 oz (90 g) g mixed pickled vegetables, drained
- ½ cup (125 g) plain mayonnaise
- 1 baguette (French loaf), sliced

Suggested wine: a light, dry white (Trebbiano di Aprilia)

Tuscan Crostini

If you have ever been to Tuscany you will recognize these delicious little fresh pâté crostini immediately. They are ubiquitous in Tuscan homes and trattorias. Always use fresh chicken livers; any good butcher or supermarket counter will have them.

Trim any connective tissue and discolored parts from the chicken livers and chop into small pieces.

Finely chop the anchovy fillets and capers together.

Melt 2 tablespoons of butter in a frying pan over medium heat. Add the onion and sauté until softened, 3–4 minutes.

Add the chicken livers and sauté for 5 minutes. Season with salt and pepper. Add the wine and simmer over low heat for 15 minutes, stirring frequently. If the mixture dries out, moisten with the stock.

Remove from the heat and chop finely in a food processor or with a large knife.

Heat the oil in a frying pan over medium heat and add the liver mixture, anchovies, and capers. Stir well, add the remaining butter, and simmer for 3–4 minutes.

Spread on the toasted bread and serve immediately.

12 oz (350 g) fresh chicken livers
4 anchovy fillets
1 tablespoon salt-cured capers
3 tablespoons (45 g) butter
1 onion, finely chopped
2 tablespoons (30 ml) dry white wine
$1/4$ cup (60 ml) extra-virgin olive oil
Salt and freshly ground black pepper
2 tablespoons beef stock or water
1 baguette (French loaf), sliced and toasted

Suggested wine: a young dry red
    (Chianti Montalbano)

Mushroom Toasts

SERVES 4

PREPARATION 20 min

COOKING 25 min

DIFFICULTY level 1

Remove any grit or dirt from the mushrooms, rinse under cold running water, and pat dry with paper towels. Separate the stalks from the caps and dice only the firm, unblemished stalks. Chop the caps coarsely.

Heat the butter and oil in a large frying pan over medium heat and sauté the onion, garlic, and calamint for 3 minutes.

Add the mushrooms and season with salt and pepper. Simmer for 5 minutes, stirring continuously. Gradually stir in enough stock to keep the mixture moist but not sloppy and simmer for 8–10 minutes. Spread each toast with a generous helping of the mushroom mixture and serve.

Variation: Spread the mushroom mixture on squares of firm, cold polenta and bake in a preheated oven at 400°F (200°C/gas 6) for 10 minutes. Serve hot.

1¼ lb (600 g) fresh porcini or other wild mushrooms

2 tablespoons butter

¼ cup (60 ml) extra-virgin olive oil

½ white or Bermuda (mild) red onion, finely chopped

2 cloves garlic, finely chopped

1 tablespoon fresh calamint (or parsley or thyme), finely chopped

Salt and freshly ground black pepper

½ cup (125 ml) vegetable stock (homemade or bouillon cube)

1 baguette (French loaf), sliced and toasted

Suggested wine: a dry white (Capezzana Bianco)

Sausage Toasts

SERVES 6

PREPARATION 10 min

COOKING 5 min

DIFFICULTY level 1

Preheat the oven to 400°F (200°C/gas 6).

Squeeze the sausage meat out of the sausage skins into a medium bowl. Add the cheese and pepper and mix very thoroughly with a fork.

Spread each toast with a generous helping of the sausage and cheese. Bake until the cheese has melted and the topping is bubbling, about 5 minutes.

Serve piping hot straight from the oven.

8 oz (250 g) highly flavored fresh Italian sausages

8 oz (250 g) fresh stracchino (crescenza) cheese or a coarsely grated semi-hard stracchino cheese

Freshly ground black pepper

1 baguette (French loaf), sliced and toasted

Suggested wine: a young, dry red (Chianti dei Colli Aretini)

Stuffed Peppers

Preheat the oven to 400°F (200°C/gas 6.)

Place the bell peppers in a roasting pan, skin-side down. Bake for 5 minutes.

Meanwhile, mix the capers, garlic, bread crumbs, parsley, raisins, pine nuts, oil, salt, and pepper in a medium bowl.

Spread the mixture on the partly-cooked bell peppers. Bake until the filling begins to brown, 10–15 minutes.

Serve hot or at room temperature.

4 medium yellow bell peppers (capsicums), cut in half lengthwise, cleaned, and seeds removed

2 tablespoons salt-cured capers, rinsed and chopped

2 cloves garlic, finely chopped

4 tablespoons fine dry bread crumbs

2 tablespoons finely chopped parsley

2 tablespoons raisins, soaked in warm water for 1 hour

2 tablespoons pine nuts

$1/2$ cup (125 ml) extra-virgin olive oil

Salt and freshly ground black pepper

Suggested wine: a light, fruity white (Pinot Bianco)

Baked Tomatoes
with rice stuffing

Preheat the oven to 350°F (180°C/gas 4). Oil a 9-inch (23-cm) baking pan. Place the potatoes in the prepared pan.

Slice the bottoms off the tomatoes. Use a teaspoon to scoop out the juice and seeds and place in a bowl. Arrange the hollowed out tomatoes on the layer of potatoes. Season with salt and pepper, and drizzle with 2 tablespoons of the oil.

Place the rice in the bowl with the tomato juice and seeds. Add the parsley, basil, oregano, garlic, and half the remaining oil. Mix well and let rest for 10 minutes.

Remove and discard the garlic. Spoon the mixture into the hollow tomatoes. Replace the tomato tops and drizzle with the remaining oil.

Bake until the potatoes are cooked through and the tomatoes are lightly browned, about 1 hour. Serve hot or at room temperature.

3 large potatoes, peeled and sliced
8 medium tomatoes
Salt and freshly ground black pepper
$\frac{1}{2}$ cup (125 ml) extra-virgin olive oil
1 cup (200 g) short-grain rice
2 tablespoons finely chopped parsley
2 tablespoons finely chopped basil
1 tablespoon freshly chopped oregano
2 cloves garlic, lightly crushed but whole

Suggested wine: a smooth, dry red
   (Merlot)

SERVES 6–8

PREPARATION 35 min

COOKING 1 h

DIFFICULTY level 2

Chicken Pâté

Preheat the oven to 400°F (200°C/gas 6). Oil a 9 x 5-inch (23 x 12-cm) loaf pan. Wrap the pan in aluminum foil to make it waterproof.

Cook the green beans in a large pot of salted boiling water until just tender, 5–7 minutes. Drain well.

Preheat the broiler (grill) on a high setting. Grill the bell pepper, turning often, until charred all over. Place in a plastic bag. Seal the bag and let rest for 10 minutes. Peel and seed the bell pepper. Chop coarsely.

Chop the chicken in a food processor with the egg white and cream until smooth. Transfer to a large bowl. Add the green beans, bell pepper, and basil. Season with salt and pepper. Mix well.

Spoon the mixture into the loaf pan. Cover and place in a roasting pan half filled with water. Bake until cooked through, about 40 minutes.

Purée the anchovies in a blender with the oil and lemon juice until smooth. Serve the pâté in slices and drizzled with the anchovy sauce.

4 oz (125 g) green beans, finely chopped
1 large red bell pepper (capsicum)
1½ lb (750 g) skinless boneless chicken breasts
1 large egg white
1 cup (250 ml) heavy (double) cream
2 tablespoons finely chopped basil
Salt and freshly ground black pepper
4 salt-cured anchovy fillets
⅓ cup (90 ml) extra-virgin olive oil
Freshly squeezed juice of 1 lemon

Suggested wine: a dry red
(San Giovese di Romagna)

Liver Pâté

SERVES 8–10

PREPARATION 20 min + 2–3 h to chill

COOKING 20 min

DIFFICULTY level 1

Heat 2 tablespoons of butter and the oil in a large frying over very low heat. Add the onions and sweat for 15 minutes.

Add the liver and raise the heat to high. Sauté for 5 minutes. Season with salt just before removing from the pan.

Chop the liver mixture in a food processor until smooth. Stir into the remaining butter, beating vigorously with a wooden spoon until the two ingredients are smoothly blended.

Transfer the pâté to a mold and chill in the refrigerator for 2–3 hours before serving.

2 cups (500 g) butter
$^1/_2$ cup (125 ml) extra-virgin olive oil
$1^1/_4$ lb (625 g) calves' liver
$1^1/_4$ lb (625 g) white onions
2 tablespoons finely chopped parsley
Salt and freshly ground black pepper

Suggested wine: a light, dry rosé
    (Bardolino Chiaretto)

Roast Bell Peppers
with anchovies

Preheat the oven to 400°F (200°C/gas 6).

Cut the bell peppers in half lengthwise. Remove the seeds and pulpy core. Rinse under cold running water and pat dry with paper towels. Bake until the skins are wrinkled and black. Let cool. Remove the charred skins with your fingers. Cut the bell peppers into strips about 2 inches (5 cm) wide.

Choose a serving dish that will hold 4–5 layers of bell peppers and line the bottom with one layer. Crumble 4 of the anchovy fillets in a small bowl and add the garlic, parsley, capers, oregano, and oil. Drizzle a layer of this mixture over the bell peppers. Cover with another layer of bell peppers and anchovy mixture. Repeat until all the ingredients have been used.

Garnish the top layer with the remaining anchovy fillets and the basil. Set aside to marinate for at least 2 hours before serving.

2 yellow, 2 green, and 2 red bell peppers (capsicums)
8 salt-cured anchovy fillets
4 cloves garlic, finely chopped
2 tablespoons finely chopped parsley
2 tablespoons salt-cured capers
$1/2$ teaspoon dried oregano
$1/4$ cup (60 ml) extra-virgin olive oil
8 fresh basil leaves, torn

Wine: a light dry red (Chianti Classico Novello)

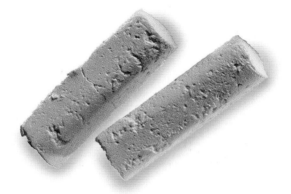

Fruit Balls
with cheese and vegetables

Shape the goat cheese into marble-size balls. Roll them in a dish filled with the chopped herbs until well coated. Set aside.

Use a small melon baller to make small balls from the cantaloupe and cucumber. Sprinkle the cantaloupe balls with 1 tablespoon of orange juice and dust with the black pepper. Drizzle the cucumber balls with salt and 1 tablespoon of oil.

Wash, dry, and remove the stems from the tomatoes. Wash, dry, and trim the radishes, cutting off roots and leaves. Wash and dry the grapes (and peel if preferred).

Line a large serving bowl with grape leaves or fresh spinach leaves. Arrange the cheese, vegetables, and fruit on top.

Drizzle with the remaining oil and orange juice just before serving.

5 oz (150 g) soft fresh goat cheese
4 tablespoons finely chopped fresh herbs
    (parsley, chives, mint, thyme, marjoram,
    tarragon, dill, basil)
1 small cantaloupe (rock melon),
    about 12 oz (350 g)
1 cucumber, peeled
Freshly squeezed juice of 1 orange
Salt and freshly ground black pepper
12 cherry tomatoes
6 small radishes
$1/4$ cup (60 ml) extra-virgin olive oil
5 oz (150 g) purple grapes
Fresh spinach or grape leaves, to serve

Wine: a dry sparkling white
    (Prosecco di Conegliano)

SERVES 4–6

PREPARATION 25 min + 1 h to chill

COOKING 30 min

DIFFICULTY level 1

Filled Pears
with gorgonzola cheese

Wash the pears thoroughly, dry well, and remove the cores with a corer. Brush the cavities with the juice of 1 lemon.

Combine the Gorgonzola cheese and cream in a bowl and mix until smooth.

Stuff the pears with the cheese mixture, pressing it down so that the cavities are completely filled.

Place in the cold part of the refrigerator for at least 1 hour.

Combine the oil, remaining lemon juice, chopped mint, salt, and pepper in a bowl and whisk until well mixed.

Use a sharp knife to cut the pears in thin round slices. Arrange the rounds on individual serving dishes and spoon the sauce over the top. Garnish with sprigs of mint and serve.

4 large ripe eating pears
Freshly squeezed juice of 2 lemons
5 oz (150 g) Gorgonzola cheese
2 tablespoons light (single) cream
$\frac{1}{4}$ cup (60 ml) extra-virgin olive oil
1 tablespoon finely chopped mint,
    + sprigs to garnish
Salt and freshly ground white pepper

Suggested wine: a dry, fruity white
    (Pinot Grigio)

Filled Rice Balls

Place the mushrooms in a small bowl and cover with warm water. Leave to soften for about 20 minutes.

Place the cold water, 4 chopped tomatoes, three-quarters of the butter, and salt in a large saucepan. Bring to a boil and add the rice. Stir frequently and simmer until the rice is tender, about 15 minutes.

Remove from the heat and stir in the Parmesan and eggs. Spread the mixture out on a large plate to cool.

In the meantime, drain the mushrooms and chop coarsely. Heat the remaining butter in a small frying pan over medium heat and sauté the mushrooms with the onion, celery, beef, chicken livers, and prosciutto for 4–5 minutes.

Add the remaining chopped tomato and season with salt. Cover and simmer over low heat until the sauce has reduced, about 20 minutes. Stir frequently so that that it doesn't stick.

Use a tablespoon to scoop up some rice and shape it into a ball about the size of an egg. Make a hollow in the ball of rice and fill with the meat sauce and one or two cubes of cheese. Seal with a little more rice.

Roll the filled rice ball in the bread crumbs and set it aside on a plate. Repeat until all the rice, meat sauce, and cheese have been used.

Heat the oil in a deep fryer or frying pan until very hot. Fry the rice balls in batches until crisp and golden brown all over.

Drain on paper towels and serve immediately.

2 tablespoons dried porcini mushrooms

2 cups (500 ml) cold water

5 large, very ripe tomatoes, peeled

$\frac{1}{2}$ cup (125 g) butter, chopped

Salt

$1\frac{3}{4}$ cups (350 g) short-grain rice

$\frac{1}{2}$ cup (60 g) freshly grated Parmesan cheese

2 large eggs

1 small onion, finely chopped

1 stalk celery, finely chopped

$1\frac{1}{4}$ cups (150 g) ground (minced) beef

4 chicken livers, finely chopped

$\frac{1}{2}$ cup (60 g) finely chopped prosciutto

$3\frac{1}{2}$ oz (100 g) mozzarella cheese, diced in $\frac{1}{2}$-inch (1-cm) cubes

Scant 2 cups (100 g) fresh bread crumbs

2 cups (500 ml) olive oil, for frying

Suggested wine: a dry red (Vignanello Rosso)

Stuffed Olives

Sauté the beef and pork in a frying pan with the olive oil for 5 minutes. Add the tomato paste and simmer for 15 minutes. Add the chicken livers and cook for 5 minutes more.

Remove from heat and chop the meat very finely in a food processor.

Return to the frying pan.

Soak the bread roll in cold water, squeeze out excess moisture, and crumble. Add the bread, one of the eggs, the Parmesan, salt, pepper, nutmeg, and cinnamon to the meat mixture. Mix well with a fork and then stuff the pitted olives.

Set out three bowls; fill the first with the flour; the second with 2 beaten eggs; and the third with the bread crumbs. Dredge the olives in the flour, dip them in the egg, and roll them in the bread crumbs. Remove excess crumbs by rolling them in your hands.

Heat the oil in a deep-fryer or frying pan until very hot. Fry the olives in small batches until a crisp, golden crust forms around each olive, 5–7 minutes each batch. Remove with a slotted spoon and drain on paper towels.

Garnish with slices of lemon and parsley and serve hot.

5 oz (150 g) pork, coarsely chopped

5 oz (150 g) beef, coarsely chopped

1/4 cup (60 ml) extra-virgin olive oil

2 tablespoons tomato paste

3 1/2 oz (100 g) chicken livers, coarsely chopped

1 day-old bread roll

3 eggs

4 tablespoons freshly grated Parmesan cheese

Salt and freshly ground black pepper

Dash each of nutmeg and cinnamon

1 1/2 lb (750 g) giant green olives, pitted

1 cup (150 g) all-purpose (plain) flour

2 cups (300 g) fine dry bread crumbs

2 cups (500 ml) olive oil, for frying

1 lemon, sliced

8 sprigs parsley

Suggested wine: a dry red (Rosso Conero)

PIZZA & FOCACCIA

Pizza Margherita

Place the fresh or active dry yeast in a small bowl and add half the warm water. Stir gently until the yeast has dissolved. Set aside for 15 minutes.

Place the flour and salt in a large bowl. Pour in the yeast mixture and most of the remaining water and stir well. Place the dough on a lightly floured work surface and knead gently and with the lightest possible touch until the dough is smooth and elastic, about 10 minutes.

Shape into a ball and place in a large oiled bowl. Set aside to rise until doubled in volume, about 1 hour 30 minutes.

Preheat the oven to 450°F (225°C/gas 7). Oil a 12-inch (30-cm) pizza pan.

When the rising time has elapsed, knead the dough for 1 minute on a lightly floured work surface.

Place in the prepared pan and use your fingertips to spread over the base of the pan. Spread the tomatoes evenly over the top, cover with the mozzarella and sprinkle with the salt and Parmesan, if using. Drizzle with 1 tablespoon of oil.

Bake until the base is golden brown and the mozzarella is melted and bubbling, 15–20 minutes.

Garnish with the basil, drizzle with the remaining oil, and serve hot.

Pizza Dough

1 oz (30 g) fresh yeast or 2 (1/4-oz/7-g) packages active dry yeast

About 2/3 cup (150 ml) warm water

3 cups (450 g) all-purpose (plain) flour

1/2 teaspoon salt

Topping

1 (14-oz/400-g) can tomatoes, chopped,

8 oz (250 g) mozzarella cheese, thinly sliced

Salt

1 tablespoon Parmesan cheese, freshly grated (optional)

3 tablespoons extra-virgin olive oil

Fresh basil leaves, torn

Suggested wine: a dry rosé (Lacryma Christi)

Quick Mini Pizzas

Preheat the oven to 400°F (200°C/gas 6). Oil a large baking sheet.

Roll out the pastry (if it is not already rolled in sheets) and use a plain cookie cutter or glass to cut out rounds.

Place the rounds, well spaced, on the prepared baking sheet. Top with a teaspoon of chopped tomato, a slice of tomato, a few cubes of mozzarella, capers, garlic, and basil. Season with salt, pepper, and oregano.

Bake until golden brown, about 15 minutes.

Transfer to a serving dish and garnish with the tomato. Serve hot or at room temperature.

14 oz (400 g) frozen puff pastry, thawed
2 large tomatoes, finely chopped
1 large tomato, sliced
5 oz (150 g) mozzarella cheese, cubed
1 tablespoon salt-cured capers, rinsed and drained
2 cloves garlic, finely sliced
Leaves from 2 sprigs basil, torn
Salt and freshly ground black pepper
2 teaspoons finely chopped oregano

Suggested wine: a light dry red (Chianti Novello)

SERVES 2–4

PREPARATION 20 min + 1 h 30 min to rise

COOKING 15–20 min

DIFFICULTY level 1

Tomato Pizza
with zucchini flowers

Prepare the pizza dough and set aside to rise.

Preheat the oven to 450°F (225°C/gas 7). Oil a 12-inch (30-cm) pizza pan.

When the rising time has elapsed, knead the dough for 1 minute on a lightly floured work surface.

Place in the prepared pan and use your fingertips to spread over the base of the pan. Cover with the mozzarella and season with salt and pepper. Drizzle with the oil.

Bake until the base is pale golden brown and the mozzarella is melted and bubbling, about 15 minutes. Add the zucchini flowers and tomatoes and bake for 5 more minutes.

Serve hot.

1 quantity pizza dough (see page 42)
6 oz (180 g) mozzarella cheese, sliced
Salt and freshly ground black pepper
1 tablespoon extra-virgin olive oil
4–6 large zucchini (courgette) flowers, rinsed and dried
8–10 cherry tomatoes, halved

Suggested wine: a dry white (Isonzo Chardonnay)

Eggplant Pizza

Prepare the pizza dough and set aside to rise.

Cut the eggplant into thin slices and brush lightly with half the oil. Grill on a hot griddle, turning frequently until the flesh is cooked, about 5 minutes. Sprinkle with salt, garlic, and parsley. Set aside.

Preheat the oven to 450°F (225°C/gas 7). Oil an 8 x 12-inch (20 x 30-cm) rectangular pizza pan.

When the rising time has elapsed, knead the dough on a lightly floured work surface for 1 minute. Place in the prepared pan, spreading evenly over the bottom. Spread with the tomatoes and top with the mozzarella. Drizzle with 1 tablespoon of oil.

Bake for 10–15 minutes. Cover with the slices of eggplant and cook for 5 more minutes. When cooked, sprinkle with the basil, drizzle with the remaining oil and serve hot.

1 quantity pizza dough (see page 42)
1 medium eggplant (aubergine)
1/4 cup (60 ml) extra-virgin olive oil
Salt
2 cloves garlic, finely chopped
2 tablespoons finely chopped parsley
12 oz (350 g) canned tomatoes, drained and chopped
6 oz (180 g) mozzarella cheese, diced
8 leaves fresh basil, torn

Suggested wine: a dry rosé
(Colli Altotiberini Rosato)

SERVES 2–4

PREPARATION 30 min + 1 h to rise

COOKING 15–20 min

DIFFICULTY level 1

Pizza
with four-cheese topping

Prepare the pizza dough and set aside to rise.

Preheat the oven to 450°F (225°C/gas 7). Oil an 8 x 12-inch (20 x 30-cm) rectangular pizza pan.

When the rising time has elapsed, knead the dough on a lightly floured work surface for 1 minute. Place in the prepared pan, spreading evenly over the bottom.

Spread with the cheeses and drizzle with the oil.

Bake until the base is browned and the cheeses are melted and bubbling, 15–20 minutes. Serve hot.

1 quantity pizza dough (see page 42)
5 oz (150 g) mozzarella cheese, diced
4 oz (125 g) Gorgonzola cheese, diced
2 oz (60 g) Emmental cheese, thinly sliced
4 tablespoons freshly grated Parmesan cheese
1 tablespoon extra-virgin olive oil

Suggested wine: a dry red (Pignoletto)

SERVES 2–4

PREPARATION 30 min + 1 h 30 to rise

COOKING 20–25 min

DIFFICULTY level 1

Spicy Pizza
with salami and black olives

Prepare the pizza dough and set aside to rise.

Preheat the oven to 450°F (225°C/gas 7). Oil an 8 x 12-inch (20 x 30-cm) rectangular pizza pan.

Knead the risen pizza dough briefly on a lightly floured work surface then press it into the prepared pan using your fingertips. Arrange the salami, olives, tomatoes, and onions on top of the dough. Season with salt and pepper. Drizzle with the oil and sprinkle with oregano.

Bake until the topping is cooked and the base is crisp and golden brown, 20–25 minutes. Serve hot.

1 quantity pizza dough (see page 42)
6 oz (180 g) spicy salami, thinly sliced
12 black olives, pitted
10 cherry tomatoes, sliced
4 small white onions, thinly sliced
Salt and freshly ground black pepper
1/4 cup (60 ml) extra-virgin olive oil
1 teaspoon dried oregano

Suggested wine: a dry red
    (Circeo Sangiovese)

SERVES 2–4

PREPARATION 30 min + 1 h 30 min to rise

COOKING 20–25 min

DIFFICULTY level 1

Tomato Pizza
with onion and pesto

Prepare the pizza dough and set aside to rise.

Preheat the oven to 450°F (225°C/gas 7). Oil two 8-inch (20-cm) pizza pans.

Pesto: Chop the basil and garlic with a pinch of salt in a food processor. Add the pine nuts, Parmesan, and pecorino and chop until smooth. Stir the oil in by hand. The pesto should be smooth and fairly dense.

Roll out the pizza dough on a lightly floured work surface into two 8-inch (20-cm) disks. Place in the prepared pans. Spread evenly with the tomatoes. Season with salt.

Bake for 10 minutes. Add the onions, sprinkling them evenly over the two pizzas. Bake until the base is crisp and the onions are lightly browned, 10–15 minutes.

Remove from the oven and dot with the pesto. Serve hot.

1 quantity pizza dough (see page 42)

Pesto
1 large bunch basil
2 cloves garlic
Salt
2 tablespoons pine nuts
2 tablespoons freshly grated Parmesan cheese
2 tablespoons freshly grated pecorino cheese
½ cup (125 ml) extra-virgin olive oil

1 (14-oz/400-g) can tomatoes, chopped, with juice
Salt
4 small white onions, finely sliced

Suggested wine: a dry white (Cinque Terre)

SERVES 2–4

PREPARATION 30 min + 1 h 30 min to rise

COOKING 25–30 min

DIFFICULTY level 1

Cheese Pizza
with onion and apple

Prepare the pizza dough and set aside to rise.

Preheat the oven to 450°F (225°C/gas 7). Oil an 8 x 12-inch (20 x 30-cm) rectangular pizza pan.

Melt the butter in a large frying pan over medium heat. Add the onions and garlic and sauté until softened, about 5 minutes. Add the brandy and sauté until it has evaporated, about 2 minutes. Stir in the cream and simmer for 2 minutes. Season with salt and pepper. Remove from heat.

Thinly slice the apples and brush with lemon juice.

Knead the risen pizza dough briefly on a lightly floured work surface then press it into the prepared pan using your fingertips. Spread with the onion mixture. Top with the Fontina, mozzarella, and apples. Season with salt and decorate with walnuts.

Bake until the base is crisp and golden brown and the topping is lightly browned, 25–30 minutes. Serve hot.

1 quantity pizza dough (see page 42)
1/4 cup (60 g) butter
2 large onions, sliced
2 cloves garlic, thinly sliced
1/4 cup (60 ml) brandy
1/4 cup (60 ml) heavy (double) cream
Salt and freshly ground black pepper
2 large Granny Smith or other tart apples, peeled and cored
Freshly squeezed juice of 1/2 lemon
5 oz (150 g) Fontina or other mild firm cheese, thinly sliced
4 oz (125 g) fresh mozzarella cheese, drained and cut into small cubes
8 walnuts, halved

Suggested wine: a dry white
(Colli di Luni Bianco)

Pizza
with ham and mushrooms

SERVES 2–4

PREPARATION 30 min + 1 h 30 min to rise

COOKING 20–25 min

DIFFICULTY level 1

Prepare the pizza dough and set aside to rise.

Preheat the oven to 450°F (225°C/gas 7). Oil a 12-inch (30-cm) pizza pan.

Knead the risen pizza dough briefly on a lightly floured work surface then press it into the prepared pan using your fingertips. Spread with the tomatoes, ham, and mushrooms. Season with salt and pepper. Drizzle with the oil.

Bake for 15 minutes. Top with the mozzarella and bake until the cheese is melted and the base is crisp and golden brown, 5–10 minutes.

Serve hot or at room temperature.

1 quantity pizza dough (see page 42)
1 (14-oz/400-g) can tomatoes, chopped, with juice
4 oz (125 g) ham, chopped
12 mushrooms preserved in oil, quartered
Salt and freshly ground black pepper
2 tablespoons extra-virgin olive oil
5 oz (150 g) fresh mozzarella cheese, drained and sliced

Suggested wine: a dry sparkling red (Lambrusco di Sorbara Rosso)

Potato Pizza
with mushrooms

Cook the potatoes in a large pot of salted boiling water until tender, about 25 minutes. Mash half the potatoes and thinly slice the rest.

Prepare the pizza dough, incorporating the mashed potatoes and 2 tablespoons of oil into the dough as you knead. Let rise for 2 hours.

Preheat the oven to 450°F (225°C/gas 7). Oil a 12-inch (30-cm) pizza pan.

Heat 2 tablespoons of oil in a large frying pan over medium heat. Add the garlic and sauté until pale gold, 3 minutes. Add the mushrooms and sauté until tender, about 5 minutes. Season with salt and pepper. Stir in the parsley and thyme.

Knead the risen pizza dough briefly on a lightly floured work surface then press it into the prepared pan using your fingertips. Spread with the sliced potatoes and mushrooms. Drizzle with the remaining oil.

Bake for 15 minutes then add the mozzarella. Bake until the base is crisp and golden brown and the mozzarella is melted, 5–10 minutes. Serve hot.

1 lb (500 g) potatoes, peeled
1 quantity pizza dough (see page 44)
1/2 cup (125 ml) extra-virgin olive oil
1 clove garlic, finely chopped
8 oz (250 g) white mushrooms, sliced
Salt and freshly ground black pepper
1 tablespoon finely chopped parsley
1 tablespoon finely chopped thyme
4 oz (125 g) fresh mozzarella cheese, drained and sliced thinly

Suggested wine: a dry white
(Colli Bolognesi Sauvignon)

SERVES 4

PREPARATION 25 min + 2 h to rise

COOKING 15–20 min

DIFFICULTY level 1

Focaccia
with extra-virgin olive oil

Prepare the pizza dough. Gradually work half the oil into the dough as you knead. Let rise in a warm place for 2 hours.

Preheat the oven to 425°F (220°C/gas 7). Oil two baking sheets.

Turn the dough out onto a lightly floured work surface and knead for 5 minutes. Divide the dough into two equal portions. Roll out each piece of dough on a lightly floured work surface to make a 12-inch (30-cm) disk.

Transfer the dough to the prepared baking sheets and fold in the edges, pinching slightly to make a border. Sprinkle with the coarse sea salt and drizzle with the remaining oil.

Bake until the focaccia is golden brown, 15–20 minutes. Serve hot or at room temperature.

1 quantity pizza dough (see page 42)
$\frac{1}{2}$ cup (125 ml) extra-virgin olive oil
1 tablespoon coarse sea salt

Suggested wine: a light, dry white
(Pinot Grigio)

SERVES 4

PREPARATION 30 min + 2 h to rise

COOKING 20–25 min

DIFFICULTY level 2

Focaccia
with cherry tomatoes and basil

Prepare the pizza dough. Gradually work half the oil into the dough as you knead. Let rise in a warm place for 2 hours.

Preheat the oven to 425°F (220°C/gas 7). Oil a 12-inch (30-cm) pizza pan.

Turn the dough out onto a lightly floured work surface and knead for 5 minutes. Press the dough into the prepared pan using your fingertips. Cover with the tomatoes. Season with salt and pepper. Drizzle with the remaining oil.

Bake until the focaccia is golden brown, 20–25 minutes. Garnish with the basil.

Serve hot or at room temperature.

1 quantity pizza dough (see page 42)
$^1/_4$ cup (60 ml) extra-virgin olive oil
12–16 cherry tomatoes, sliced
Salt and freshly ground black pepper
Fresh basil, to garnish

Suggested wine: a light, dry white
   (Alto Adige Sylvaner)

SERVES 4

PREPARATION 35 min + 1 h 30 min to rise

COOKING 35 min

DIFFICULTY level 2

Focaccia
with summer vegetables

Prepare the pizza dough and set aside to rise.

Preheat the oven to 450°F (225°C/gas 7). Oil an 8 x 12-inch (20 x 30-cm) rectangular pizza pan.

Slice the tomatoes, remove the seeds, and sprinkle with salt. Place cut side down in a colander and let drain for 10 minutes.

Sauté the garlic and zucchini in 2 tablespoons of oil in a large frying pan over medium heat for 5 minutes. Season with salt.

Place the risen dough in the pan and use your fingertips to spread it evenly over the bottom. Top with the zucchini, garlic, bell peppers, and tomatoes. Season with salt and pepper. Drizzle with the remaining oil.

Bake for about 15 minutes. Sprinkle with the olives, capers, basil, and Parmesan. Bake until golden brown, about 10 minutes more. Serve hot.

1 quantity pizza dough (see page 42)
2 large ripe tomatoes
Salt and freshly ground black pepper
1 clove garlic, lightly crushed
2 large zucchini (courgettes), sliced
1/3 cup (90 ml) extra-virgin olive oil
1 large red bell pepper (capsicum), seeded and sliced
1 large yellow bell pepper (capsicum), seeded and sliced
1/2 cup (50 g) black olives, pitted and halved
1 tablespoon salt-cured capers, rinsed and drained
Fresh basil leaves, torn
3 oz (90 g) Parmesan cheese, cut into flakes

Suggested wine: a dry white (Trentino Pinot Bianco)

SERVES 4–6

PREPARATION 15 min

COOKING 50 min

DIFFICULTY level 1

Easy Focaccia
with zucchini

Heat 3 tablespoons of the oil in a large frying pan over medium heat. Add the onion and water. Sauté until the onion is tender, about 5 minutes. Season with salt and pepper.

Preheat the oven to 350°F (180°C/gas 4). Oil a 10-inch (25-cm) springform pan.

Place the flour and baking powder in a large bowl. Add the milk, remaining oil, eggs, zucchini, and onion. Season with salt and pepper and mix well. Spoon the mixture into the prepared pan.

Bake until golden brown and a skewer inserted into the center comes out clean, about 50 minutes.

Serve hot or at room temperature.

1/3 cup (90 ml) extra-virgin olive oil
1 medium white onion, finely sliced
2 tablespoons water
Salt and freshly ground black pepper
2 cups (300 g) all-purpose (plain) flour
2 teaspoons baking powder
1/3 cup (90 ml) milk
3 large eggs, lightly beaten
4 zucchini (courgettes), cut into
    tiny cubes

Suggested wine: a light, dry white
    (Trentino Riesling Italico)

SERVES 4–6

PREPARATION 25 min + 2 h to rise

COOKING 30–35 min

DIFFICULTY level 2

Garlic Focaccia
with mortadella and cheese

Cook the potatoes in a small pot of salted boiling water until tender, about 10 minutes. Drain and mash until smooth.

Prepare the pizza dough. Gradually work the potato and 1 tablespoon of oil into the dough as you knead. Let rise for 2 hours.

Preheat the oven to 400°F (200°C/gas 6). Oil a 12-inch (30-cm) pizza pan.

Turn the dough out onto a lightly floured work surface and knead for 5 minutes. Press into the pan using your fingertips. Sprinkle with the garlic. Top with the tomatoes. Sprinkle with salt and oregano. Drizzle with the remaining oil.

Bake until golden brown, 20–25 minutes. Top with mortadella and cheese and serve hot or at room temperature.

2 large potatoes, peeled and cut into small cubes

1 quantity pizza dough (see page 42)

1/4 cup (60 ml) extra-virgin olive oil

4 cloves garlic, halved

12 cherry tomatoes, sliced

1 teaspoon dried oregano

4 oz (125 g) mortadella or ham, sliced

4 oz (125 g) Provolone or other firm mature cheese, thinly sliced

Suggested wine: a dry red (Trentino Cabernet)

SERVES 4

PREPARATION 30 min + 2 h to rise

COOKING 15–20 min

DIFFICULTY level 1

Focaccia
with prosciutto and parmesan

Prepare the pizza dough and set aside to rise.

Preheat the oven to 400°F (200°C/gas 6). Oil a 12-inch (30-cm) pizza pan.

Press dough into the pan using your fingers. Let rise for 30 minutes.

Bake until golden brown, 15–20 minutes.

Remove from the oven and top with the prosciutto, arugula, Parmesan, and tomatoes. Cut into wedges and serve hot.

- 1 quantity pizza dough (see page 42)
- 4 oz (125 g) sliced prosciutto
- 2 oz (60 g) arugula (rocket), coarsely chopped
- 3 oz (90 g) Parmesan cheese, cut into flakes
- 8–10 cherry tomatoes, halved

Suggested wine: a young, dry red (Reggiano Rosso Novello)

Filled Focaccia
with gorgonzola and bell peppers

Prepare the pizza dough and set aside to rise.

Preheat the oven to 450°F (225°C/gas 7). Oil an 8 x 12-inch (20 x 30-cm) rectangular pizza pan.

Bake the bell peppers in the oven until dark and charred all over, 20–30 minutes. Place in a brown paper bag. Close the bag and let rest for 10 minutes. Peel and seed the bell peppers. Rinse well, dry, and slice thinly.

Turn the dough out onto a lightly floured surface and knead for 5 minutes. Divide into 2 equal portions and press one portion into the prepared pan using your fingertips. Prick with a fork.

Cover with the peppers, garlic, and Gorgonzola. Season with salt and pepper and drizzle with 2 tablespoons of oil.

Roll out the remaining dough into a rectangle large enough to cover the pan. Cover the filling with the dough. Press the cherry tomatoes into the dough at regular intervals. Sprinkle with the oregano and drizzle with the remaining oil.

Bake until the focaccia is golden brown, 25–30 minutes.

Serve hot or at room temperature.

1 quantity pizza dough (see page 42)
1/4 cup (60 ml) extra-virgin olive oil
1 large red bell pepper (capsicum)
1 large yellow pepper (capsicum)
1 clove garlic, finely sliced
8 oz (250 g) Gorgonzola cheese, sliced
Salt and freshly ground black pepper
12 cherry tomatoes
1 teaspoon dried oregano

Suggested wine: a light, sparkling, dry red (Colli Piacentini Gotturnio Frizzante)

SERVES 4

PREPARATION 20 min + 1 h 30 min to rise

COOKING 20–25 min

DIFFICULTY level 1

Focaccia
with green olives, mint, and fennel

Prepare the pizza dough and set aside to rise.

Preheat the oven to 450°F (225°C/gas 7). Oil an 8 x 12-inch (20 x 30-cm) rectangular pizza pan.

Place the risen dough in the pan and use your fingertips to spread it evenly over the bottom. Sprinkle with the olives, garlic, mint, fennel seeds, red pepper flakes, and salt. Drizzle with the oil and let rise for 30 minutes.

Preheat the oven to 400°F (200°C/gas 6).

Bake until the base is golden brown, 20–25 minutes. Serve hot.

1 quantity pizza dough (see page 42)
2 cups (200 g) green olives, pitted and halved
3 cloves garlic, finely sliced
3 mint leaves, finely chopped
2 tablespoons fennel seeds
1 teaspoon red pepper flakes
Salt
3 tablespoons extra-virgin olive oil

Suggested wine: a dry, fruity white (Colli di Rimini Bianco)

SERVES 4–6

PREPARATION 35 min + 2 h 30 min to rise

COOKING 45 min

DIFFICULTY level 2

Focaccia
with leeks and bacon

Prepare the pizza dough. Gradually work 2 tablespoons of the oil into the dough as you knead. Let rise for 2 hours.

Oil an 8 x 12-inch (20 x 30-cm) rectangular pizza pan. Turn the dough out onto a floured work surface and knead for 5 minutes. Press into the prepared pan using your fingertips. Let rise for 30 minutes.

Preheat the oven to 350°F (180°C/gas 4).

Heat 2 tablespoons of the oil in a large frying pan over medium heat. Add the leeks and sauté for 3–4 minutes. Add the stock and simmer until tender, about 5 minutes. Sauté the bacon over medium heat until lightly browned. Stir the bacon and cheeses into the leeks. Season with salt. Beat the egg yolk, milk, and thyme in a small bowl.

Brush the focaccia with the remaining oil. Spread with the leek mixture. Drizzle with the egg.

Bake until golden brown, about 30 minutes. Serve hot.

1 quantity pizza dough (see page 42)
1/2 cup (125 ml) extra-virgin olive oil
5 medium leeks, finely sliced
1/4 cup (60 ml) vegetable stock
4 oz (125 g) bacon, chopped
1 cup (125 g) freshly grated Gruyère cheese
2 tablespoons freshly grated Parmesan cheese
Salt
1 large egg yolk
1/4 cup (60 ml) milk
1 tablespoon finely chopped thyme

Suggested wine: a dry red (Sangiovese di Romagna)

Cheese Focaccia
with salami

Prepare the pizza dough and set aside to rise.

Preheat the oven to 450°F (225°C/gas 7). Oil an 8 x 12-inch (20 x 30-cm) rectangular pizza pan.

Turn the dough out onto a lightly floured work surface and knead for 5 minutes. Press into the prepared pan using your fingers.

Mix together the ricotta, eggs, parsley, salami, mozzarella, Parmesan, salt, and pepper in a medium bowl. Spread over the focaccia. Drizzle with the oil.

Bake until golden brown, 20–25 minutes. Serve hot or at room temperature.

I quantity pizza dough (see page 42)
2 tablespoons extra-virgin olive oil
I cup (250 g) ricotta cheese, drained
2 large eggs, lightly beaten
2 tablespoons finely chopped parsley
2 oz (60 g) salami, chopped
2 oz (60 g) fresh mozzarella cheese, cut into small cubes
4 tablespoons freshly grated Parmesan cheese
Salt and freshly ground black pepper

Suggested wine: a dry red (Garda Barbera)

Potato Focaccia
with cheese and sausage

Cook the potatoes in a large pot of salted boiling until tender, 10–15 minutes. Drain and mash.

Prepare the pizza dough. Gradually work the potatoes, eggs, and 2 tablespoons of oil into the dough as you knead. Let rise for 3 hours.

Oil a 12-inch (30-cm) pizza or quiche pan. Roll out two-thirds of the dough on a lightly floured work surface until large enough to line the prepared pan. Line the pan with the dough. Cover with the sausage, mozzarella, Emmental, and pecorino.

Roll out the remaining dough and cut into ¾-inch (2-cm) strips using a pastry wheel. Arrange the strips over the focaccia in a lattice pattern. Brush with the remaining oil and sprinkle with the oregano. Let rise for 30 minutes.

Preheat the oven to 400°F (200°C/gas 6). Bake until the focaccia is golden brown, 35–40 minutes. Serve hot or at room temperature.

- 2 medium potatoes, peeled and cut into chunks
- 1 quantity pizza dough (see page 42)
- 2 large eggs
- ¼ cup (60 ml) extra-virgin olive oil
- Salt
- 3 Italian sausages, skinned and broken into bite-size pieces
- 5 oz (150 g) mozzarella cheese, cut into small cubes
- 10 oz (300 g) Emmental cheese, coarsely grated
- 3 tablespoons freshly grated pecorino cheese
- 1 teaspoon dried oregano

Suggested wine: a dry red (Garda Cabernet)

PASTA

SERVES 4–6

PREPARATION 15 min

COOKING 1 h 15 min

DIFFICULTY level 1

Penne
with meat sauce

Heat the butter in a large frying pan over medium heat. Add the carrot, celery, and onion and sauté until softened, about 5 minutes.

Add the pork and beef and sauté until browned, 5–7 minutes. Add the ham and cook for 1 minute. Increase the heat to high, pour in the wine, and let it evaporate, about 2 minutes. Stir in the tomatoes. Season with salt, pepper, and nutmeg. Partially cover the pan and simmer over low heat for about 1 hour.

Cook the pasta in a large pot of salted boiling water until al dente. Drain well and add to the sauce.

Add the cheese and toss well. Serve hot.

1 carrot, finely chopped
2 stalks celery, finely chopped
1 medium onion, finely chopped
2 tablespoons butter
1 lb (500 g) ground (minced) pork
5 oz (150 g) ground (minced) beef
1 cup (125 g) diced ham
2/3 cup (150 ml) dry white wine
6 large tomatoes, peeled and coarsely
    chopped
Salt and freshly ground black pepper
1/4 teaspoon freshly ground nutmeg
1 lb (500 g) penne
1/2 cup (60 g) freshly grated Parmesan
    cheese

Suggested wine: a crisp, dry red (Donnas)

SERVES 4–6

PREPARATION 10 min

COOKING 15 min

DIFFICULTY level 1

Fusilli
with pesto, cream, and tomatoes

Bring a large pot of salted water to a boil over high heat.

Mix the pesto and tomato sauce in a large bowl. Stir in the cream until well blended. Season with salt and pepper.

Cook the pasta in the boiling water until al dente.

Heat individual serving bowls with cooking water from the pasta. Discard the water.

Drain the pasta and transfer to the warmed bowls. Add the sauce, toss well, and serve hot.

½ cup (125 g) pesto (homemade — see page 54 — or storebought)
1 cup (250 ml) finely chopped, peeled tomatoes
⅓ cup (90 ml) heavy (double) cream
Salt and freshly ground black pepper
1 lb (500 g) fusilli

Suggested wine: a dry white (Trentino Bianco)

Cool Fusilli
with tomatoes and onion

Cook the pasta in a large pot of salted boiling water until al dente.

Drain and cool under cold running water. Drain again, dry in a clean cloth, and transfer to a large salad bowl.

Add 2 tablespoons of the oil and toss well. Add the tomatoes, onion, garlic, basil, chile peppers, if using, and the remaining oil. Season with salt and toss well.

Serve at room temperature or chill in the refrigerator for 30 minutes.

1 lb (500 g) fusilli

⅓ cup (90 ml) extra-virgin olive oil

1½ lb (750 g) firm ripe salad tomatoes, peeled and coarsely chopped

1 sweet red Spanish onion, finely chopped

3 tablespoons finely chopped basil

2 cloves garlic, finely chopped

1–2 dried chile peppers, crumbled (optional)

Salt

Suggested wine: a light, dry white (Grechetto)

Farfalle Salad
with cherry tomatoes and olives

Cook the pasta in a large pot of salted boiling water until al dente.

Drain and cool under cold running water. Drain again and dry on a clean cloth. Transfer to a large salad bowl.

Add 2 tablespoons of the oil and toss well. Add the tomatoes, capers, mozzarella, olives, and basil. Mix well.

Heat the remaining oil in a small frying pan over medium heat. Add the garlic and sauté until pale golden brown, 3–4 minutes. Add the anchovies and sauté, crushing with a fork, until dissolved in the oil, 3–4 minutes.

Drizzle this mixture over the salad and toss well. Chill for 30 minutes before serving.

1 lb (500 g) farfalle

1/4 cup (60 ml) extra-virgin olive oil

20 cherry tomatoes, halved

1 tablespoon capers preserved in salt, rinsed

8 oz (250 g) fresh mozzarella cheese, drained and cut into small cubes

Generous 1/2 cup (60 g) black olives, pitted

1 tablespoon finely chopped basil

2 cloves garlic, finely chopped

4 anchovy fillets preserved in oil, drained

Suggested wine: a dry white
(Torgiano Bianco)

SERVES 4–6

PREPARATION 10 min

COOKING 20 min

DIFFICULTY level 1

Farfalle
with peas and scallions

Heat the oil in a large frying pan over medium heat. Add the pancetta and spring onions. Sauté until the onions are tender and the pancetta is crisp and lightly browned, about 5 minutes.

Add the flour and mix well. Pour in the stock and wine and mix well. Bring to a boil. Add the peas and cook until the peas are tender and the sauce has thickened. Season with salt and pepper. Mix well and remove from the heat.

Meanwhile, cook the pasta in a large pan of salted, boiling water until al dente. Drain well and add to the pan with the sauce.

Sprinkle with parsley and toss over high heat for 1 minute. Serve hot.

1/4 cup (60 ml) extra-virgin olive oil
5 oz (150 g) pancetta or bacon, chopped
8 spring onions, thinly sliced
2 tablespoons all-purpose (plain) flour
1 cup (250 ml) vegetable stock (homemade or bouillon cube)
1/2 cup (125 ml) dry white wine
1 1/2 cups (250 g) frozen peas
Salt and freshly ground black pepper
1 lb (500 g) farfalle
2 tablespoons finely chopped parsley

Suggested wine: a dry white (Grecanico)

SERVES 4–6

PREPARATION 15 min + 1 h to soak

COOKING 35 min

DIFFICULTY level 1

Penne
with mussels and tomatoes

Soak the mussels in a large bowl of cold water for 1 hour. Rinse well and scrub or pull off the beards.

Heat 2 tablespoons of the oil in a large saucepan. Add the garlic and sauté until pale golden brown, 2–3 minutes. Add the mussels and cook over medium-high heat until they open, 7–10 minutes. Remove from the heat. Shell the mussels, discarding any that did not open. Filter the cooking juices through a piece of muslin and set aside.

Heat the remaining oil in a large saucepan over medium heat. Add the cooking juices from the mussels and the tomatoes and simmer for 5 minutes. Set aside while the pasta is cooking.

Cook the pasta and potatoes in a large pan of salted water until the pasta is al dente and the potatoes are tender, 10–12 minutes.

Drain well and add to the pan with the tomatoes. Add the mussels and basil, and season with salt and pepper. Toss well and sprinkle with the cheese. Garnish with basil and serve hot.

2 lb (1 kg) fresh mussels, in shell
1/4 cup (60 ml) extra-virgin olive oil
2 cloves garlic, finely chopped
1 lb (500 g) penne
1 lb (500 g) potatoes, peeled and cut into 1/2 inch (1 cm) cubes
1 lb (500 g) cherry tomatoes, halved
Leaves from 1 sprig of basil, torn + extra, to garnish
Salt and freshly ground black pepper
1/2 cup (60 g) freshly grated pecorino or Parmesan cheese

Suggested wine: a dry white (Greco di Tufo)

SERVES 4–6

PREPARATION 15 min

COOKING 15 min

DIFFICULTY level 1

Penne
with walnut sauce

Melt the butter in a frying pan over medium heat. Add the garlic and sauté until softened, 2–3 minutes. Add the walnuts and sauté for 2 minutes.

Stir in the cream. Simmer over low heat until the sauce thickens, about 12 minutes. Season with salt and white pepper.

Meanwhile, cook the pasta in a large pan of salted, boiling water until al dente. Drain well and add to the pan with the walnut sauce.

Toss gently for 30 seconds. Sprinkle with the marjoram and serve hot.

5 tablespoons butter
2 cloves garlic, finely chopped
40 walnuts, coarsely chopped
1 cup (250 ml) heavy (double) cream
Salt and freshly ground white pepper
1 lb (500 g) penne rigate
2 tablespoons finely chopped marjoram

Suggested wine: a light, dry white
(Capri Bianco)

Penne
with gorgonzola and cream

Heat the butter and Gorgonzola with the cream in a double boiler over barely simmering water until the cheese has melted. Season with salt, 5–7 minutes.

Meanwhile, cook the pasta in a large pan of salted, boiling water until al dente. Drain and add to the cheese mixture. Mix well so that the pasta is coated with the sauce. Add the marjoram and Parmesan.

Serve hot.

$1/4$ cup (60 g) butter
12 oz (350 g) Gorgonzola cheese, crumbled
$2/3$ cup (150 ml) heavy (double) cream
Salt
1 lb (500 g) penne
Sprigs of fresh marjoram
$1/2$ cup (60 g) freshly grated Parmesan cheese

Suggested wine: a dry rosé (Vesuvio Rosato)

Spaghetti
with tomato sauce

SERVES 4–6

PREPARATION 20 min

COOKING 50 min

DIFFICULTY level 1

Cook the tomatoes with the salt in a covered saucepan over medium heat for 5 minutes. Add the onion, garlic, basil, oil, sugar, and salt. Partially cover and simmer over low heat until the sauce is reduced, about 40 minutes.

Remove from the heat and run through a food mill or process in a food processor or blender until smooth.

Cook the spaghetti in a large pan of salted, boiling water until al dente.

Place in a heated serving bowl and toss with the sauce. Serve hot.

3 lb (1.5 kg) firm-ripe tomatoes, peeled and coarsely chopped

Salt

1 red onion, thinly sliced

2 cloves garlic, finely chopped

Leaves from 1 small bunch basil, torn

2 tablespoons extra-virgin olive oil

$\frac{1}{2}$ teaspoon sugar

1 lb (500 g) spaghetti

Suggested wine: a dry white (Costa d'Amalfi Bianco)

Spaghetti
with lemons and black olives

Beat together the oil, lemon zest, lemon juice, black olives, garlic, and basil in a large bowl. Season with salt and pepper.

Cook the pasta in a large pan of salted, boiling water until al dente. Drain well and add to the bowl with the sauce. Toss well. Transfer to a serving dish. Serve hot.

½ cup (125 ml) extra-virgin olive oil

Zest of 2 lemons, cut into julienne strips

Freshly squeezed juice of 2 lemons

1½ cups (150 g) pitted black olives, coarsely chopped

2 cloves garlic, finely chopped

16 basil leaves, torn

Salt and freshly ground black pepper

1 lb (500 g) spaghetti

Suggested wine: a dry white
    (Lamezia Greco)

SERVES 4–6

PREPARATION 20 min

COOKING 20 min

DIFFICULTY level 1

Spaghettini
with mint, garlic, and olives

Heat the oil in a large frying pan over medium heat until pale gold, about 3 minutes. Add the anchovies and sauté—crushing with a fork—until they have dissolved into the oil, about 5 minutes. Remove from the heat and add the mint and parsley.

Meanwhile, cook the pasta in a large pan of salted, boiling water until al dente.

Drain and add to the sauce. Sprinkle with the capers and olives, toss well, and serve hot.

2 cloves garlic, lightly crushed but whole

$^1/_3$ cup (90 ml) extra-virgin olive oil

6 salt-cured anchovy fillets, finely chopped

2 tablespoons finely chopped mint

4 tablespoons finely chopped parsley

1 lb (500 g) spaghettini

2 tablespoons capers preserved in brine, rinsed

16 black olives, pitted and chopped

Suggested wine: a dry white (Prosecco)

SERVES 4–6

PREPARATION 15 min

COOKING 15 min

DIFFICULTY level 1

Spaghetti
alla carbonara

Sauté the onion in the oil in a small saucepan over medium heat until lightly browned, 2–3 minutes. Add the bacon and sauté until crisp, about 5 minutes. Remove from the heat and set aside.

Beat the egg yolks and cream in a large bowl. Season with salt and pepper and sprinkle with the Parmesan.

Cook the pasta in a large pan of salted, boiling water until al dente.

Drain and add to the bacon. Return to high heat, add the egg mixture, and toss the briefly so that the eggs cook lightly but are still creamy.

Serve immediately.

1 onion, finely chopped
1/4 cup (60 ml) extra-virgin olive oil
1 1/3 cups (160 g) diced bacon
6 large eggs
1/3 cup (90 ml) heavy (double) cream
Salt and freshly ground black pepper
3/4 cup (90 g) freshly grated pecorino
   or Parmesan cheese
1 lb (500 g) spaghetti

Suggested wine: a light, dry rosé
   (Castelli Romani Rosato)

SERVES 4–6

PREPARATION 30 min + 1 h to drain

COOKING 1 h

DIFFICULTY level 1

Spaghetti
with fried eggplant and tomato

Place the eggplant slices in a colander and sprinkle with the coarse sea salt. Let drain for 1 hour. Shake off as much salt as possible.

Heat the oil in a large deep frying pan until very hot. Fry the eggplant in small batches until golden brown, 5–7 minutes per batch. Drain on paper towels.

Tomato Sauce: Stir together the tomatoes, onion, garlic, basil, oil, sugar, and salt in a medium saucepan. Cover and simmer over medium heat until the tomatoes have broken down, about 15 minutes. Uncover and simmer over low heat until reduced, about 40 minutes. Transfer to a food processor and chop until smooth.

Meanwhile, cook the pasta in a large pot of salted boiling water until al dente. Drain and add to the sauce. Toss well.

Top with the fried eggplant and sprinkle with the Parmesan, if liked. Serve hot.

- 1 lb (500 g) eggplant (aubergine); thinly sliced
- 2 tablespoons coarse sea salt
- 1 cup (250 ml) olive oil, for frying

Tomato Sauce
- 2 lb (1 kg) firm-ripe tomatoes, peeled and coarsely chopped
- 1 red onion, thinly sliced
- 2 cloves garlic, finely chopped
- Leaves from 1 small bunch basil, torn
- 2 tablespoons extra-virgin olive oil
- $1/4$ teaspoon sugar
- Salt
- 1 lb (500 g) spaghetti or bucatini

- 1 cup (125 g) freshly grated Parmesan cheese (optional)

Suggested wine: a dry white (Contessa Entellina Bianco)

SERVES 4–6

PREPARATION 15 min

COOKING 1 h

DIFFICULTY level 1

Orecchiette
with meat sauce

Heat the oil in a large saucepan over medium heat. Add the onions and sauté until softened, 3–4 minutes.

Add the meat and sauté until browned all over, about 5 minutes. Add the tomatoes, celery, and basil. Season with salt and pepper. Cover and simmer over low heat for about 1 hour.

Cook the pasta in a large pot of salted boiling water until al dente. Drain well and then add to the sauce.

Toss well over high heat for 1 minute. Sprinkle with the pecorino or Parmesan and serve hot.

1/3 cup (90 ml) extra-virgin olive oil
2 large onions, finely chopped
1 lb (500 g) lean ground (minced) beef, lamb, or pork
1 lb (500 g) tomatoes, peeled and chopped
2 stalks celery, finely chopped
2 tablespoons finely chopped basil
1 lb (500 g) fresh orecchiette
Salt and freshly ground black pepper
1/2 cup (60 g) freshly grated pecorino or Parmesan cheese

Suggested wine: a dry red
   (Gioa del Colle Rosso)

SERVES 4–6

PREPARATION 40 min

COOKING 3 h 20 min

DIFFICULTY level 2

Spaghetti
with meatballs

Sauce: Sauté the onion and carrot in the oil in a large frying pan over medium heat until softened, about 5 minutes. Add the beef and sauté until browned all over, 8–10 minutes.

Add the tomatoes and season with salt. Simmer over low heat until the meat is very tender, about 3 hours. Remove the meat. It can be served separately after the pasta.

Meatballs: Mix the veal, egg, Parmesan, bread crumbs, and nutmeg in a large bowl until well blended. Shape the mixture into balls the size of marbles.

Heat the frying oil in a large frying pan. Fry the meatballs in small batches until golden brown, 5–7 minutes. Drain on paper towels.

Cook the pasta in a large pot of salted boiling water until al dente. Drain and add to the pan with the sauce. Toss with the meatballs and serve hot.

If preferred, make a quicker version of this southern Italian recipe by replacing the sauce with the simpler tomato sauce on page 98.

Sauce
1 small onion, finely chopped
1 carrot, finely chopped
1/4 cup (60 ml) extra-virgin olive oil
12 oz (350 g) beef, in a single cut
2 lb (1 kg) ripe tomatoes, peeled and chopped
Salt

Meatballs
12 oz (350 g) ground (minced) beef
1 egg
2 cups (250 g) freshly grated Parmesan cheese
4 cups (250 g) fresh bread crumbs
1/4 teaspoon freshly grated nutmeg
1 cup (250 ml) olive oil, for frying

1 lb (500 g) spaghetti

Suggested wine: a dry red (Rosso Piceno)

Tagliatelle
with peas and pancetta

Melt ¼ cup (60 g) of the butter in a large frying pan over medium heat. Add the onion, pancetta, and garlic and sauté until softened, about 5 minutes.

Add the peas and season with salt, pepper, and sugar. Pour in the water, cover, and simmer for 10 minutes. Uncover and simmer until the sauce has reduced by half, about 10 minutes.

Cook the pasta in the boiling water until al dente, 3–4 minutes. Drain and add to the sauce.

Toss with the remaining butter, Parmesan, and parsley. Serve hot.

14 oz (400 g) fresh tagliatelle
⅓ cup (90 g) butter
1 onion, finely chopped
½ cup (60 g) diced pancetta (or bacon)
1 clove garlic, finely chopped
2 cups (300 g) frozen peas
Salt and freshly ground white pepper
⅛ teaspoon sugar
2 cups (500 ml) hot water
½ cup (60 g) freshly grated
   Parmesan cheese
1 tablespoon finely chopped parsley

Suggested wine: a smooth, dry white
   (Friuli Grave Bianco)

Paglia and Fieno
with gorgonzola cheese

Melt the butter in a medium saucepan over low heat and add the Gorgonzola and cream. Season with salt and pepper. Simmer over low heat, stirring constantly, until the cheese has melted.

Cook the pasta in a large pan of salted, boiling water until al dente, 3–4 minutes. Drain the pasta and transfer to a heated serving dish.

Add the Gorgonzola sauce, tossing carefully with two forks. Sprinkle with the Parmesan and serve hot.

14 oz (400 g) paglia e fieno (mixture of spinach and plain tagliatelle)

1/4 cup (60 g) butter

8 oz (250 g) Gorgonzola cheese, cut into small cubes

2/3 cup (150 ml) heavy (double) cream

Salt and freshly ground white pepper

4 tablespoons freshly grated Parmesan cheese

Suggested wine: a dry, aromatic white (Friuli Isonzo Traminer Aromatico)

Tagliatelle
with roasted tomato sauce

Preheat the oven to 400°F (200°C/gas 6).

Cut the tomatoes in half and squeeze out the seeds. Place the tomato shells upside-down on a baking sheet. Bake until the tomatoes have lost their excess water and the skins are burnt, 20–25 minutes.

Let cool a little then slip off the skins and mash the flesh in a large bowl. Stir in the garlic, oil, parsley, and salt.

Cook the pasta in a large pot of salted boiling water until al dente, 3–4 minutes.

Drain well and place in a heated serving dish. Add the sauce, toss gently, and serve hot.

14 oz (400 g) fresh tagliatelle
2 lb (1 kg) firm-ripe tomatoes
2 cloves garlic, finely chopped
1/3 cup (90 ml) extra-virgin olive oil
1 tablespoon finely chopped parsley
Salt

Suggested wine: a dry white
    (Colli Berici Garganega)

SERVES 4

PREPARATION 10 min

COOKING 15 min

DIFFICULTY level 2

Tagliatelle
with cream and ham

Melt the butter in a large frying pan over medium heat. Add the ham and sauté until crisp, about 5 minutes.

Pour in the cream and simmer for 5 minutes. Season with salt, pepper, and nutmeg.

Cook the pasta in a large pan of salted, boiling water until al dente, 3–4 minutes.

Drain and add to the pan with the sauce. Simmer and toss gently until the pasta is well flavored with the sauce.

Sprinkle with the Parmesan and serve hot.

14 oz (400 g) fresh tagliatelle
4 oz (125 g) ham, cut into thin strips
$1/4$ cup (60 g) butter
Generous $3/4$ cup (200 g) heavy (double) cream
Salt and freshly ground white pepper
$1/8$ teaspoon freshly grated nutmeg
$1/2$ cup (60 g) freshly grated Parmesan cheese

Suggested wine: a dry white
(Colli di Conegliano)

SERVES 4

PREPARATION 40 min + 1 h to make pasta

COOKING 40 min

DIFFICULTY level 2

Pasta Squares
with tomato and pancetta

Pasta Dough: Place the flour, cornmeal, and salt on a clean work surface and make a well in the center. Mix in enough water to make a smooth dough. Knead until smooth and elastic, 15–20 minutes. Shape the dough into a ball, wrap in plastic wrap (cling film), and let rest for 30 minutes.

Roll out the dough to a thickness of $1/8$ inch (3 mm). Cut into $3/4$-inch (2-cm) squares.

Sauce: Sweat the onion and pancetta in the oil in a small frying pan over low heat until the onion has softened, about 10 minutes.

Stir in the tomatoes, season with salt and pepper, and simmer over low heat for 25 minutes.

Bring a large pot of salted water to a boil over high heat. Cook the pasta in the boiling water until al dente, 3–4 minutes.

Drain and add to the sauce, tossing gently. Sprinkle with the pecorino and serve hot.

Pasta Dough

- 2 cups (300 g) all-purpose (plain) flour
- $2/3$ cup (100 g) fine polenta (stoneground cornmeal)
- $1/2$ teaspoon salt
- $2/3$ cup (150 ml) lukewarm water + more, as needed

Sauce

- 1 red onion, finely chopped
- 5 oz (150 g) pancetta or bacon
- 2 tablespoons extra-virgin olive oil
- $1\frac{1}{2}$ lb (750 g) tomatoes, peeled and chopped and pressed through a fine mesh strainer (passata)
- Salt and freshly ground black pepper
- 4 tablespoons freshly grated aged pecorino cheese

Suggested wine: a smooth, dry red (Colli Euganei Merlot)

Classic Lasagne

Meat Sauce: Melt the butter in a medium saucepan over medium heat. Add the prosciutto, onion, carrot, and celery. Sauté until the vegetables have softened, about 5 minutes.

Add the beef and sauté until lightly browned, about 5 minutes. Add the wine and simmer until it evaporates. Add the tomato and stock. Mix well and season with salt. Cover and simmer over low heat for 2 hours. Stir the sauce from time to time and add a little more stock if it begins to stick to the pan.

Béchamel Sauce: Melt the butter in a large saucepan over medium heat. Add the flour and stir until smooth. Remove from the heat and add the milk all at once, mixing well to prevent lumps from forming. Return the saucepan to the heat and simmer, stirring constantly, until thickened and cooked, 5–7 minutes. Season with salt and pepper.

Preheat the oven to 400°F (200°C/gas 6).

Blanch the lasagne sheets in small batches in a large pan of salted boiling water with 1 tablespoon of oil. Scoop out with a slotted spoon, squeeze gently, and let dry on a clean cloth.

Butter a large ovenproof dish and spread a little of the Béchamel over the bottom. Place a layer of lasagna on top. Spoon a little of the meat sauce over the lasagna and then add a layer of the Béchamel sauce. Sprinkle with a little of the Parmesan. Add another layer of pasta and repeat until all the ingredients are in the dish. Sprinkle with the Parmesan and dot with the remaining butter.

Bake until golden brown and bubbling, about 20 minutes.

Let rest for 5 minutes. Serve hot.

Meat Sauce
1/3 cup (90 g) butter
8 oz (250 g) prosciutto, finely chopped
1 medium onion, finely chopped
1 medium carrot, finely chopped
1 small stalk celery, finely chopped
12 oz (350 g) lean ground (minced) beef
1/3 cup (90 ml) dry white wine
1 large tomato, peeled and chopped
1/2 cup (125 ml) beef stock
    (homemade or bouillon cube)
Salt

Béchamel Sauce
1/4 cup (60 g) butter
1/3 cup (50 g) all-purpose (plain) flour
2 cups (500 ml) milk
Salt and freshly ground black pepper

14 oz (400 g) fresh lasagna sheets
1 tablespoon extra-virgin olive oil
1 1/4 cups (150 g) freshly grated Parmesan
    cheese
2 tablespoons butter

Suggested wine: a dry red
    (Sangiovese di Romagna)

Ravioli
with tomato sauce

Pasta Dough: Sift the flour onto a work surface and make a well in the center. Add the eggs and enough water to make a smooth dough. Roll out the dough using a pasta machine or by hand. Cut into long sheets about 4-inches (10-cm) wide.

Filling: Mix the ricotta, eggs, sugar, parsley, lemon zest, bread crumbs, nutmeg, cinnamon, salt, and pepper until well blended.

Place heaped teaspoons of the filling down the center of the sheets of pasta at intervals of about 2 inches (5 cm). Moisten the edges of the dough and fold over to seal, pressing down gently between the mounds of filling. Use a sharp knife or a wheel cutter (for fluted edges) to cut between the mounds.

Tomato Sauce: Heat the oil in a large frying pan over medium heat. Stir in the tomatoes and garlic. Season with salt and pepper. Simmer until the sauce has reduced, about 10 minutes. Remove the garlic and add the parsley and butter.

Cook the pasta in small batches in a large pot of salted boiling water until al dente, 3–4 minutes. Use a slotted spoon to transfer to serving plates. Spoon the sauce over the top and sprinkle with the Parmesan and basil. Serve hot.

Pasta Dough
3 cups (450 g) all-purpose (plain) flour
2 eggs
1/3 cup (90 ml) water

Filling
1 2/3 cups (400 g) ricotta cheese, drained
2 eggs, lightly beaten
1/3 cup (70 g) sugar
1 tablespoon finely chopped parsley
Finely grated zest of 1/2 lemon
1/2 cup (60 g) fine dry bread crumbs
1/8 teaspoon nutmeg
1/4 teaspoon cinnamon
Salt and freshly ground white pepper

Tomato Sauce
3 tablespoons extra-virgin olive oil
2 lb (1 kg) tomatoes, peeled and chopped
1 clove garlic, peeled
1 tablespoon finely chopped parsley
2 tablespoons butter
2 tablespoons freshly grated Parmesan cheese
4 leaves basil, torn

Suggested wine: a dry white (Vernaccia di Oristano)

RISOTTO, GNOCCHI, & POLENTA

SERVES 4

PREPARATION 15 min

COOKING 20 min

DIFFICULTY level 1

Rice
with peas and pesto

Boil the rice in 8 cups (2 liters) of salted boiling water until tender, about 15 minutes.

Boil the peas in salted water until tender, about 5 minutes.

Melt the butter in a large frying pan over medium heat and sauté the onion until softened, 3–4 minutes.

Drain the rice and peas and add to pan with the onion. Season with salt and pepper, add the parsley, and sauté over high heat for 1–2 minutes.

Place in a heated serving dish and spoon the pesto over the top. Serve hot.

2 cups (400 g) short-grain rice
1 cup (150 g) frozen peas
1/3 cup (90 g butter)
1 onion, finely chopped
Salt and freshly ground black pepper
2 tablespoons finely chopped parsley
1 quantity pesto (see page 52)

Suggested wine: a dry white (Vermentino)

SERVES 4

PREPARATION 15 min

COOKING 55 min

DIFFICULTY level 2

Risotto
with spring vegetables

Remove the tough outer leaves from the artichokes. Cut off the top third of the leaves. Cut in half and scrape out any fuzzy inner core. Slice finely. Place in a bowl of water with the lemon juice.

Heat 2 tablespoons of oil in a large frying pan over medium heat. Add the garlic and sauté until pale gold, 2–3 minutes. Discard the garlic. Add the mushrooms and sauté for 5 minutes. Drain the artichokes and add to the pan. Sauté until tender, about 10 minutes.

Meanwhile, heat 2 tablespoons of oil in another large frying pan over medium heat. Add half the onion and sauté until transparent, 3–4 minutes. Add the zucchini, asparagus, peas, bell pepper, and tomatoes. Season with salt and pepper. Cook until tender, 6–8 minutes.

Heat the remaining oil in a large frying pan over medium heat. Add the remaining onion and sauté until transparent, 3–4 minutes. Add the rice and sauté for 2 minutes. Begin adding the stock, 1/2 cup (125 ml) at a time, cooking and stirring until each addition has been absorbed and the rice is tender, 15–18 minutes. Stir in the vegetables, butter, and Parmesan. Garnish with the parsley and serve hot.

2 artichokes

Juice of 1 lemon

2 small tomatoes, peeled and chopped

1/3 cup (90 ml) extra-virgin olive oil

1 clove garlic, lightly crushed but whole

5 oz (150 g) button mushrooms, sliced

2 small onions, finely chopped

4 medium zucchini (courgettes), cut into small cubes

12 asparagus tips, cut into short sections

1 cup (150 g) fresh or frozen peas

1 small yellow bell pepper (capsicum), seeded and chopped

Salt and freshly ground black pepper

1 3/4 cups (350 g) risotto rice

3 cups (750 ml) boiling chicken stock (homemade or bouillon cube)

1/4 cup (60 g) butter, cut into pieces

1/2 cup (60 g) freshly grated Parmesan

1 tablespoon finely chopped parsley

Suggested wine: a dry white (Orvieto Classico)

Risotto
with spinach and bacon

Cook the spinach in salted boiling water until tender, 3–4 minutes. Drain, squeeze out excess moisture, and chop finely.

Melt ¼ cup (60 g) of butter in a large frying pan over medium heat. Add the onion and sauté until transparent, 3–4 minutes. Add the rice and sauté for 2 minutes. Add ½ cup (125 ml) of the stock and cook until it is absorbed. Add the spinach and mix well. Keep adding the stock, ½ cup (125 ml) at a time, cooking and stirring until each addition has been absorbed and the rice is tender, 15–18 minutes.

Cook the bacon in a small frying pan over medium heat until crisp, about 5 minutes.

Season the risotto with pepper and stir in the remaining butter and the Parmesan. Remove from the heat, cover, and let rest for 2 minutes.

Spoon the risotto into serving dishes and top each portion with slices of bacon. Serve hot.

1 lb (500 g) fresh or frozen spinach
Salt
⅓ cup (90 g) butter
1 small onion, finely chopped
1¾ cups (350 g) risotto rice
3 cups (750 ml) boiling vegetable stock, (homemade or bouillon cube)
8–12 slices bacon
Freshly ground black pepper
½ cup (60 g) freshly grated Parmesan

Suggested wine: a smooth, dry red (Garda Merlot)

SERVES 4

PREPARATION 15 min

COOKING 40 min

DIFFICULTY level 1

Risotto
with tomato and fresh basil

Melt 2 tablespoons of the butter in a medium saucepan over medium heat. Add the onion and sauté until softened, 3–4 minutes. Add the tomatoes and mix well. Simmer until the tomatoes have broken down and the sauce is thickened, about 15 minutes.

Melt 2 tablespoons of the remaining butter in a large frying pan over high heat. Add the rice and sauté for 2 minutes. Lower heat to medium. Pour in the wine and cook until it evaporates. Stir in the tomato sauce and basil.

Begin adding the stock, 1/2 cup (125 ml) at a time, cooking and stirring until each addition has been absorbed and the rice is tender, 15–18 minutes.

Stir in the remaining butter and the Parmesan. Season with salt and pepper. Remove from the heat and let rest for 1 minute. Garnish with the extra basil and serve hot.

1/3 cup (90 g) butter

1 small onion, finely chopped

2 cups (500 g) peeled and chopped tomatoes

2 cups (400 g) risotto rice

1/3 cup (90 ml) dry white wine

3 cups (750 ml) boiling vegetable stock (homemade or bouillon cube)

20 basil leaves, torn + extra, to garnish

1/4 cup (30 g) freshly grated Parmesan cheese

Salt and freshly ground black pepper

Suggested wine: a dry white (Cinque Terre)

SERVES 4

PREPARATION 15 min

COOKING 35 min

DIFFICULTY level 1

Risotto
with bell peppers

Heat the oil in a large frying pan over medium heat. Add the onion and garlic and sauté until the onion is transparent, 3–4 minutes. Add the bell peppers and sauté until tender, 5–7 minutes.

Add the rice and sauté for 2 minutes. Stir in the wine and cook until it evaporates, 2–3 minutes.

Begin adding the stock, 1/2 cup (125 ml) at a time, cooking and stirring until each addition has been absorbed and the rice is tender, 15–18 minutes.

Season with salt and mix well. Remove from the heat and stir in the basil, parsley, and cilantro. Cover and let rest for 1 minute. Garnish with the basil and serve hot.

- 1/4 cup (60 ml) extra-virgin olive oil
- 1 large onion, finely chopped
- 1 clove garlic, finely chopped
- 2 large red bell peppers (capsicums), seeded and thinly sliced
- 2 large yellow bell peppers (capsicums), seeded and thinly sliced
- 1 3/4 cups (350 g) risotto rice
- 1/3 cup (90 ml) dry white wine
- 3 cups (750 ml) boiling vegetable stock (homemade or bouillon cube)
- Salt
- 1 tablespoon finely chopped basil + extra, to garnish
- 1 tablespoon finely chopped parsley
- 1 tablespoon finely chopped cilantro (coriander)

Suggested wine: a dry white (Franciacorta Bianco)

SERVES 4

PREPARATION 10 min

COOKING 25 min

DIFFICULTY level 2

Risotto
with apples and zucchini

Place the apples in a bowl. Drizzle with the lemon juice.

Heat the oil in a large frying pan over medium heat. Add the onion and sauté until transparent, 3–4 minutes. Add the potatoes, zucchini, and carrot. Sauté for 2 minutes.

Add the rice and sauté for 2 minutes. Add ½ cup (125 ml) of the stock and stir until it is absorbed. Add the apples and lemon juice and mix well. Keep adding the stock, ½ cup (125 ml) at a time, cooking and stirring until each addition has been absorbed and the rice is tender, 15–18 minutes.

Remove from the heat and stir in the soy sauce, curry powder, dill, and saffron. Season with salt and pepper and mix gently.

Remove from the heat, cover and let rest for 1 minute. Garnish with dill and serve hot.

2 green apples, cored and thinly sliced

Freshly squeezed juice of 1 lemon

2 tablespoons extra-virgin olive oil

1 large onion, finely chopped

4 medium potatoes, peeled and cut into small cubes

3 medium zucchini (courgettes), cut into small cubes

1 large carrot, cut into small cubes

1¾ cups (350 g) risotto rice

3 cups (750 ml) boiling vegetable stock (homemade or bouillon cube)

1 teaspoon dark soy sauce

1 teaspoon curry powder

2 tablespoons finely chopped dill + extra, to garnish

Pinch of saffron strands

Salt and freshly ground black pepper

Suggested wine: a dry white (Pinot Grigio)

Risotto
with potato and cabbage

Heat 3 tablespoons of oil in a small frying pan over medium heat. Add the potatoes and sauté until tender and golden brown, 8–10 minutes. Remove from the heat.

Heat the remaining oil in a large frying pan over medium heat. Add the rice and sauté for 2 minutes. Pour in the wine and cook until it evaporates, 2–3 minutes. Add the onion and cabbage and sauté for 3 minutes.

Begin adding the stock ½ cup (125 ml) at a time, cooking and stirring until each addition has been absorbed and the rice is tender, 15–18 minutes.

Add the potatoes. Season with salt and mix well. Garnish with the parsley and serve hot.

⅓ cup (90 ml) extra-virgin olive oil

2 large potatoes, peeled and cut into small cubes

1¾ cups (350 g) risotto rice

⅓ cup (90 ml) dry white wine

1 large onion, chopped finely

8 oz (250 g) cabbage, shredded

3 cups (750 ml) boiling vegetable stock (homemade or bouillon cube)

Salt

1 tablespoon finely chopped parsley, to garnish

Suggested wine: a light dry red (Bardolino)

SERVES 4
PREPARATION 15 min
COOKING 50 min
DIFFICULTY level 2

Risotto
with leeks and fontina

Heat the honey in a small saucepan over medium heat until it begins to caramelize, 3–4 minutes. Add the wine and let it reduce over medium heat until the sauce is thick, about 15 minutes. Remove from the heat and cover.

Melt ¼ cup (60 g) of butter in a large frying pan over medium heat. Add the leeks and sauté until transparent, 3–4 minutes. Add the rice and sauté for 2 minutes. Begin adding the stock, ½ cup (125 ml) at a time, cooking and stirring until each addition has been absorbed and the rice is tender, 15–18 minutes.

Season with salt and pepper and mix well. Remove from the heat. Add the remaining butter and the Fontina. Drizzle with the honey and wine sauce and serve hot.

3 tablespoons honey
2 cups (500 ml) fruity red wine
⅓ cup (90 g) butter
4 small leeks, cleaned and finely sliced
1¾ cups (350 g) risotto rice
3 cups (750 ml) boiling beef stock (homemade or bouillon cube)
Salt and freshly ground black pepper
3 oz (90 g) Fontina or other mild firm cheese, cut into small cubes

Suggested wine: a dry red (Barbera d'Asti)

SERVES 4

PREPARATION 10 min

COOKING 25 min

DIFFICULTY level 1

Risotto
with prosecco and cilantro

Melt 2 tablespoons of the butter in a large frying pan over medium heat. Add the onion and sauté until transparent, 3–4 minutes.

Add the rice and sauté for 2 minutes. Pour in the prosecco and cook until it evaporates, about 3 minutes. Begin adding the stock, ½ cup (125 ml) at a time, cooking and stirring until each addition has been absorbed and the rice is tender, 15–18 minutes.

Season with salt and pepper. Remove from the heat. Stir in the remaining butter. Cover and let rest for 1 minute.

Sprinkle with the cilantro and Parmesan. Serve hot.

¼ cup (60 g) butter

1 large onion, finely chopped

1¾ cups (350 g) risotto rice

¾ cup (200 ml) prosecco (or champagne)

3 cups (750 ml) boiling chicken stock (homemade or bouillon cube)

Salt and freshly ground black pepper

2 tablespoons finely chopped cilantro (coriander)

3 oz (90 g) Parmesan cheese, cut into flakes

Suggested wine: a dry sparkling white (Prosecco di Conegliano)

SERVES 4

PREPARATION 10 min

COOKING 25 min

DIFFICULTY level 1

Risotto
with smoked salmon

Warm 1 tablespoon of the oil in a small frying pan over medium-low heat. Add the salmon and sauté for 1 minute. Add the cream and mix gently. Remove from the heat and set aside.

Heat the remaining oil in a large frying pan over medium heat. Add the spring onions and sauté until they begin to soften, about 2 minutes.

Add the rice and sauté for 2 minutes. Pour in wine and cook until it evaporates. Begin adding the stock, 1/2 cup (125 ml) at a time, cooking and stirring until each addition has been absorbed and the rice is tender, 15–18 minutes.

Season with salt and pepper. Add the salmon and cream and mix well. Remove from the heat and let rest for 1 minute.

Garnish with the parsley and serve hot.

3 tablespoons extra-virgin olive oil

4 oz (125 g) smoked salmon, cut into in very small pieces

1 cup (250 ml) heavy (double) cream

2 spring onions, chopped

1¾ cups (350 g) short-grain rice

1/3 cup (90 ml) dry white wine

3 cups (750 ml) boiling vegetable stock (homemade or bouillon cube)

Salt and freshly ground black pepper

1–2 tablespoons finely chopped parsley, to garnish

Suggested wine: a dry sparkling white (Prosecco di Conegliano)

Potato Gnocchi
with butter and sage

Gnocchi: Cook the potatoes in a large pot of salted boiling water until tender, 20–25 minutes. Drain and slip off their skins. Mash until smooth.

Gradually stir in the egg yolks, salt, and enough flour to obtain a smooth dough. Take a piece of dough and roll it on a lightly floured work surface into a rope about ½-inch (1-cm) in diameter. Cut into pieces about 1 inch (2.5 cm) long. Repeat until all the dough is used. To give the gnocchi their special grooves, twist around the tines of a fork.

Place the gnocchi on a clean kitchen towel and let rest for 1 hour.

Set a large pot of salted water to boil. Cook the gnocchi in batches. Lower the first batch (20–24 gnocchi) gently into the boiling water. After a few minutes they will rise to the surface. Simmer for 1–2 minutes, then scoop out with a slotted spoon. Place in a heated serving dish. Repeat until all the gnocchi are cooked.

Melt the butter with the sage and drizzle over the gnocchi. Sprinkle with the Parmesan and serve hot.

Potato Gnocchi
2 lb (1 kg) starchy potatoes, with peel
2 large egg yolks
Salt
2 cups (300 g) all-purpose (plain) flour

Sauce

½ cup (125 g) butter, melted
6–8 leaves fresh sage
1 cup (150 g) freshly grated Parmesan cheese

Suggested wine: a dry white (Piave Tocai Italico)

SERVES 6–8

PREPARATION 15 min

COOKING 35 min

DIFFICULTY level 1

Pumpkin Gnocchi

Preheat the oven to 400°F (200°C/gas 6). Place the pumpkin on a baking sheet and bake until tender, 15–20 minutes. Place in a bowl while still hot and mash until smooth. Let cool for 10–15 minutes.

Stir in the flour, eggs, and salt. Combine very thoroughly until the mixture is smooth and firm, adding a little more flour if necessary.

Bring a large pot of salted water to a boil. Shape the dough into balls about the size of walnuts. Drop them into the water a few at a time and cook for 2–3 minutes. Remove with a slotted spoon and place in a heated serving dish. Repeat until all the gnocchi are cooked.

Drizzle with melted butter, sprinkle with the Parmesan, and serve hot.

3 lb (1.5 kg) pumpkin, peeled and coarsely chopped
3 cups (450 g) all-purpose (plain) flour
2 eggs
Salt
1/2 cup (125 g) butter
1/2 cup (60 g) freshly grated Parmesan cheese

Suggested wine: a dry red (Garda Corvino)

Spinach Gnocchi
with tomato sauce

Melt the butter in a small saucepan and add the tomato sauce. Simmer over low heat for 5 minutes. Remove from the heat and set aside.

Gnocchi: Mix the ricotta and spinach in a large bowl. Add the eggs, 1 cup (125 g) of Parmesan, and ½ cup (75 g) of flour. Season with salt and pepper and add the lemon zest.

Dust your hands with the remaining flour and form the mixture into 2-inch (5-cm) balls.

Cook the gnocchi in a large pot of salted boiling water until they rise to the surface, about 5 minutes. Remove with a slotted spoon and place in a heated serving dish.

Cover with the tomato sauce and sprinkle with the remaining Parmesan. Serve hot.

¼ cup (60 g) butter

2 cups (500 ml) storebought or homemade tomato sauce (see page 94)

Gnocchi

2 cups (500 g) fresh ricotta, strained through a fine mesh

1½ cups (350 g) finely chopped cooked spinach, drained

2 large eggs

1 cup (125 g) + 2 tablespoons freshly grated Parmesan cheese

1 cup (150 g) all-purpose (plain) flour

Salt and freshly ground black pepper

Grated zest of ½ lemon

Suggested wine: a dry white (Breganze Pinto Grigio)

SERVES 4–6

PREPARATION 25 min + time to make gnocchi

COOKING 45 min

DIFFICULTY level 2

Potato Gnocchi
with gorgonzola and tomato sauce

Prepare the potato gnocchi.

Melt the butter in a large frying pan over medium heat. Add the garlic and tomatoes and simmer over low heat for 15 minutes.

Melt the Gorgonzola in a heavy-based saucepan over very low heat.

Add the melted Gorgonzola to the tomatoes.

Cook the gnocchi in small batches in a large pot of salted boiling water following the instructions on page 134.

Transfer the cooked gnocchi to the frying pan with the sauce using a slotted spoon. Mix well over high heat for 1 minute. Sprinkle with the Parmesan and serve hot.

1 quantity potato gnocchi (see page 134)
1/4 cup (60 g) butter
1 clove garlic, finely chopped
1 quart (1 liter) tomato passato (sieved tomatoes)
5 oz (150 g) Gorgonzola cheese, crumbled
1/2 cup (60 g) freshly grated Parmesan cheese

Suggested wine: a dry white (Bianco di Custoza)

SERVES 4

PREPARATION 30 min

COOKING 45 min

DIFFICULTY level 2

Brown Gnocchi
with cheese fondue sauce

Place the cheese in a bowl and cover with the milk. Leave to soak.

Cook the potatoes in a large pot of salted boiling water until tender, 20–25 minutes. Drain and mash until smooth.

Place in a large bowl. Gradually stir in both flours. Season with salt and pepper. Mix well to make a smooth dough.

Knead the dough on a lightly floured work surface until smooth, 3–4 minutes. Roll the dough into ropes about ¾-inch (2 cm) in diameter. Cut into pieces about 1 inch (2.5 cm) long. Lay on a lightly floured clean cloth to dry.

Place the cheese and 3 tablespoons of the milk in a double boiler over barely simmering water. Add the butter and stir until the cheese has melted, about 5 minutes. Stir in the egg yolks one at a time.

Cook, stirring constantly, until the sauce is thick, about 5 minutes. Season with salt and pepper.

Cook the gnocchi in small batches in a large pot of salted boiling water until they rise to the surface. Scoop out with a slotted spoon and place in a large heated serving bowl.

Pour the cheese fondue sauce over the top. Mix gently and serve hot.

14 oz (400 g) Fontina or other mild cheese suitable for melting, sliced
⅔ cup (150 ml) milk
2 lb (1 kg) starchy potatoes, peeled
⅔ cup (100 g) all-purpose (plain) flour
⅔ cup (100 g) buckwheat flour
Salt and freshly ground black pepper
1 tablespoon butter
2 large egg yolks, lightly beaten

Suggested wine: a dry red (Fumin)

SERVES 4–6

PREPARATION 10 min + 1 h to cool

COOKING 1 h

DIFFICULTY level 1

Polenta Gnocchi

Bring the milk to a boil in a large heavy-bottomed saucepan. Pour in the cornmeal and stir continuously with a long-handled wooden spoon to prevent lumps forming. Season with salt, pepper, and nutmeg. Add one-third of the butter. Stir energetically for about 45 minutes.

Remove from the heat and add 2 tablespoons of the Parmesan, the egg yolks and milk, and ham. Dampen a clean work surface and pour the polenta onto it. Spread to about ½-inch (1-cm) thick. Let cool for 1 hour.

Preheat the oven to 400°F (200°C/gas 6). Use a cookie cutter or glass about 2½-inches (6-cm) in diameter to cut out disks.

Grease a rectangular ovenproof dish with butter and arrange the disks in overlapping layers.

Heat the remaining butter and pour over the top. Sprinkle with the remaining Parmesan. Bake until the topping is golden brown, about 15 minutes. Serve hot.

1 quart (1 liter) milk
2 cups (300 g) polenta
   (stoneground cornmeal)
Salt and freshly ground white pepper
Pinch of nutmeg
⅔ cup (150 g) butter
1 cup (125 g) freshly grated Parmesan
   cheese
3 egg yolks, beaten with 1 tablespoon milk
½ cup (60 g) ham, coarsely chopped

Suggested wine: a dry red
   (Bardolino Classico)

Semolina Gnocchi

Bring the milk to a boil in a large, heavy-based saucepan. Sprinkle the semolina in little by little, stirring all the time so that no lumps form. Keep stirring energetically until the mixture is smooth and dense, about 30 minutes.

Remove from the heat and season with salt. Stir in half the butter, the egg yolks, half the Parmesan, and the Gruyère. Spread to about ½-inch (1-cm) thick on a lightly floured work surface. Let cool.

Preheat the oven to 350°F (180°C/gas 4). Use a cookie cutter or glass about 2½-inches (6-cm) in diameter to cut out disks. Butter an ovenproof dish and use the pieces leftover after cutting out the disks to form a first layer. Sprinkle with a little of the remaining Parmesan. Lay the disks over the top, one overlapping the next.

Melt the remaining butter and pour over the top. Sprinkle with the remaining Parmesan and a grinding of pepper. Bake until golden brown, about 30 minutes. Serve hot.

1 quart (1 liter) milk
1⅔ cups (250 g) semolina
Salt and freshly ground white pepper
½ cup (125 g) butter
2 egg yolks
1 cup (125 g) freshly grated Parmesan cheese, + more Parmesan to serve separately at the table
3 tablespoons freshly grated Gruyère cheese

Suggested wine: a light, dry rosé (Frusinate Rosato)

SERVES 6

PREPARATION 10 min

COOKING 50 min

DIFFICULTY level 1

Polenta
with sausage sauce

Melt the lard in a large frying pan and sauté the onion, celery, carrot, and parsley over a medium heat until the vegetables have softened, about 5 minutes.

Add the tomato paste and water, season with salt, then cover the pan and simmer over low heat for 30 minutes.

Peel the sausage and chop coarsely. Add to the vegetables and simmer for 15 minutes more.

Meanwhile prepare the polenta: bring the water to a boil with the sea salt. Gradually sprinkle in the polenta while stirring continuously with a large balloon whisk to stop lumps from forming.

Cook over low heat, stirring continuously for about 40 minutes. When cooked, turn out onto a polenta board (or large serving platter) and spoon the sauce over the top. Serve hot.

3 tablespoons lard (or butter)
1 onion, finely chopped
1 stalk celery, finely chopped
1 small carrot, finely chopped
2 tablespoons finely chopped parsley
1 tablespoon concentrated tomato paste dissolved in 1/2 cup (125 ml) cold water

Salt

12 oz (300 g) Italian sausage
3 quarts (3 liters) cold water
1 tablespoon coarse sea salt
3 1/4 cups (500 g) polenta (stoneground cornmeal)

Suggested wine: a young, full-bodied red (Sangiovese di Aprilia)

SERVES 4

PREPARATION 15 min

COOKING 1 h

DIFFICULTY level 1

Polenta
with leek sauce

Bring the water to a boil with the salt. Gradually sprinkle in the polenta while stirring continuously with a large wooden spoon to stop lumps from forming. Cook over a low heat, stirring continuously for about 45 minutes.

Cut the prepared leeks into ⅛ in (2–3 mm) thick slices.

Melt the butter in a saucepan over medium heat, then add the leeks. Cover and simmer gently for until wilted, about 5 minutes.

Season with salt and white pepper. Add the cream and milk and simmer for 20–25 minutes.

When the polenta is done (it should be very thick, almost stiff), turn it out onto a heated serving platter. Serve hot with the leek sauce handed round separately in another heated serving dish.

- 1½ quarts (1.5 liters) cold water
- 1 tablespoon coarse salt
- 2⅓ cups (350 g) polenta (stoneground cornmeal)
- 12 oz (350 g) leeks, prepared net weight, white part only
- 3 tablespoons butter
- Salt and freshly ground white pepper
- 1¼ cups (300 ml) light (single) cream
- 4–5 tablespoons whole milk

Suggested wine: a dry, lightly sparkling red (Barbera del Monferrato Vivace)

SERVES 6–8

PREPARATION 10 min

COOKING 30 min

DIFFICULTY level 1

Baked Polenta
with tomato cheese topping

Prepare the tomato sauce. Prepare the polenta. Turn the polenta out onto a board or clean work surface and let cool.

Preheat the oven to 400°F (200°C/gas 6). Oil an ovenproof baking dish.

Slice the polenta and arrange the slices in the prepared dish. Spoon the tomato sauce over the top. Top with the cheese and anchovies, if using.

Bake until the cheese is melted, about 15 minutes.

1 quantity tomato sauce (seepage 92)
1 quantity polenta (see page 146)
1 tablespoon extra-virgin olive oil
10 oz (300 g) mild Provolone cheese, diced
Anchovy fillets (optional)

Suggested wine: a light, dry red
   (San Colombano)

SOUPS

Italian Soup
with garbanzo beans

Bring the water with the garbanzo beans to a boil in a large saucepan over medium-low heat. Skim off the froth. Cook over low heat until the beans are very soft, about 2 hours. Season with salt and remove from the heat (there should still be plenty of cooking water). Drain, reserving the cooking water.

Cook the cardoons in salted boiling water until tender, 25–30 minutes (or 10–15 minutes, if using celery). Drain and set aside.

Sauté the mushrooms and sausage in the oil in a large saucepan over medium heat until the sausage is browned all over, about 10 minutes. Sprinkle with the flour and season with salt and pepper. Pour in 6 cups (1.5 liters) of the reserved cooking water. Cover and simmer over medium heat for 30 minutes.

Stir in the cooked garbanzo beans and cardoons. Add the pasta and cook until al dente, 5–7 minutes. Serve hot.

- 4 quarts (4 liters) water, + more as required
- 2 cups (300 g) dried garbanzo beans (chickpeas), soaked overnight
- Salt
- 1 lb (500 g) cardoons or celery stalks, tough strings removed and coarsely chopped
- 1 oz (30 g) dried mushrooms, soaked in warm water for 15 minutes
- 2 Italian sausages, crumbled
- 1/3 cup (90 ml) extra-virgin olive oil
- 1 teaspoon all-purpose (plain) flour
- Freshly ground black pepper
- 12 oz (350 g) small dried soup pasta, such as ditalini

Suggested wine: a young, dry red (Chianti)

Broccoli Soup

Roman cauliflower is a beautiful emerald green and the florets are pointed rather than rounded as in white cauliflower. If you can't find it in your local market, use ordinary green broccoli in its place.

Separate the florets from the core of the broccoli, keeping the tender inner leaves. Rinse thoroughly and boil until just tender, 5–7 minutes in a pot of salted, boiling water.

Toast the bread, rub with the garlic, and place in individual soup bowls.

When the cauliflower is cooked, pour a half ladleful of the cooking water over each slice of toast. Arrange the florets and leaves, well drained, on the toasted bread.

Drizzle with the oil and lemon juice and season with salt and pepper. Serve hot.

2 lb (1 kg) Roman cauliflower (or green broccoli)
4 thick slices firm-textured bread
2 cloves garlic
1/2 cup (125 ml) extra-virgin olive oil
2 tablespoons freshly squeezed lemon juice
Salt and freshly ground white pepper

Suggested wine: a dry white (Savuto)

Pasta Soup
with vegetables and pesto

Pesto: Chop the basil, pine nuts, and garlic in a food processor until smooth. Add the cheese and oil and mix well.

Soup: Bring the stock to a boil in a large saucepan over medium heat. Add the green beans and potatoes. Season with salt and pepper and simmer for 15 minutes.

Add the pasta and cook until al dente and the vegetables are very tender, 5–7 minutes.

Add the pesto and mix well. Ladle into serving bowls. Serve hot.

Pesto
2 oz (60 g) basil leaves
1/4 cup (45 g) pine kernels
2 cloves garlic
1/2 cup (60 g) freshly grated Parmesan
1/3 cup (90 ml) extra-virgin olive oil

Soup
2 quarts (2 liters) vegetable stock
   (homemade or bouillon cube)
12 oz (350 g) green beans,
   cut in short lengths
2 large waxy (boiling) potatoes, peeled and
   cut into small cubes
Salt and freshly ground black pepper
8 oz (250 g) farfalline or other small
   soup pasta

Suggested wine: a dry, fruity white
   (Golfo del Tigullio Bianco)

SERVES 4

PREPARATION 40 min

COOKING 30 min

DIFFICULTY level 1

Bread Dumplings
in beef stock

Soak the bread in the milk until softened, about 10 minutes. Drain, squeezing out the excess milk.

Sauté the onion in 2 tablespoons of butter in a small frying pan over low heat until very soft and golden, about 20 minutes. Season with salt, remove from the heat, and let cool.

Use a wooden spoon to beat the remaining butter in a large bowl until softened. Add the soaked bread to the butter with the sautéed onion, flour, 1 tablespoon of the parsley, eggs, and nutmeg. Form the mixture into walnut-sized dumplings.

Simmer the dumplings in a large pot with the stock until cooked, about 7 minutes. Sprinkle with the remaining parsley and serve hot.

- 1 lb (500 g) day-old bread, crusts removed and crumbled
- 1¼ cups (300 ml) milk
- 1 onion, finely chopped
- ⅓ cup (90 g) butter
- Salt
- ¾ cup (125 g) all-purpose (plain) flour
- 1 small bunch parsley, finely chopped
- 5 large eggs
- ⅛ teaspoon freshly grated nutmeg
- 1 quart (1 liter) boiling beef stock (homemade or bouillon cube)

Suggested wine: a dry white (Friuli Pinot Grigio)

Fresh Pasta
in beef stock

Pasta Dough: Place the flour, salt, and nutmeg in a mound on a work surface and make a well in the center. Break the eggs into the well and use a fork to mix in. Stir in the Parmesan to make a smooth dough. Knead until smooth and elastic, 15–20 minutes. Shape the dough into a ball, wrap in plastic wrap (cling film), and let rest for 10 minutes.

Divide the dough into four and roll out to a thickness of about $3/4$ inch (2 cm). Let dry on a kitchen cloth for 10 minutes. Cut the slices finely until the pasta resembles grains of rice. Spread out on a clean surface and let dry in a dry, airy place for at least 1 hour.

Bring the stock to a boil and cook the pasta until al dente, 1–2 minutes. Sprinkle with Parmesan and serve hot.

Pasta Dough
$2^2/_3$ cups (400 g) all-purpose (plain) flour
$1/_4$ teaspoon salt
$1/_8$ teaspoon freshly grated nutmeg
3 tablespoons freshly grated Parmesan
4 eggs

To Serve
2 quarts (2 liters) beef stock
   (homemade or bouillon cube)
$3/_4$ cup (90 g) freshly grated Parmesan

Suggested wine: a dry white
   (Breganze Chardonnay)

Bread Soup
with tomato and bell peppers

Preheat the broiler (grill) on a high setting. Grill the bell peppers, turning them from time to time, until they are charred all over. Remove from the grill and transfer to a plastic bag. Seal the bag and let rest for 10 minutes. Remove the peppers from the bag. Peel them, then discard the seeds. Slice the peppers finely.

Heat the oil in a large saucepan over medium heat. Add the garlic and sauté until pale golden brown, 2–3 minutes. Add the tomatoes and half the bell peppers. Bring to a boil. Add the bread and mix well. Add the stock and mix well. Season with black pepper and bring to a boil. Simmer until the bread has broken down, about 15 minutes. Season with salt and add the basil and marjoram.

Ladle into serving bowls and top with the remaining peppers. Garnish with the basil. Serve hot.

3 large red bell peppers (capsicums)

$\frac{1}{4}$ cup (60 ml) extra-virgin olive oil

2 cloves garlic, finely chopped

$1\frac{1}{2}$ lb (750 g) ripe tomatoes, chopped

8 oz (250 g) crusty white bread, preferably unsalted

3 cups (750 ml) vegetable stock (homemade or bouillon cube)

Salt and freshly ground black pepper

2 tablespoons finely chopped basil, + extra leaves, to garnish

2 tablespoons finely chopped marjoram

Suggested wine: a young, dry red (Chianti Novello)

Vegetable Soup
with fresh garlic

Blanch the tomatoes in boiling water for 2 minutes. Drain and peel them. Chop coarsely.

Heat the oil in a large saucepan over low heat. Add the onion and sauté until softened, 3–4 minutes. Add the cabbage, lettuce, Swiss chard, celery, carrots, potatoes, and tomatoes. Mix well and simmer until the vegetables begin to soften, about 10 minutes. Add the stock and season with pepper. Bring to a boil, cover, and simmer until the vegetables are very tender, about 20 minutes.

Melt the butter in a large frying pan over medium heat. Add the bread and fry until golden brown on both sides, about 5 minutes. Drain on paper towels.

Add the peas to the soup and simmer for 5 minutes. Add the garlic and parsley, and mix well. Check the seasoning.

Arrange the fried bread in serving bowls. Ladle the soup over the top. Sprinkle with the cheese and serve hot.

12 oz (350 g) tomatoes
1/4 cup (60 ml) extra virgin olive oil
1 medium onion, finely sliced
12 oz (350 g) Savoy cabbage, shredded
10 lettuce leaves, shredded
10 Swiss chard (silver beet) leaves, shredded
1 stalk celery, finely sliced
4 medium potatoes, peeled and thinly sliced
2 large carrots, thinly sliced
1 quart (1 liter) vegetable stock
   (homemade or bouillon cube)
Freshly ground black pepper
1/3 cup (90 g) butter
4 large slices crusty white bread
1 1/2 cups (250 g) frozen peas
5 cloves garlic, very finely chopped
3 tablespoons finely chopped parsley
1/4 cup (30 g) freshly grated Parmesan
   cheese

Suggested wine: a dry red
   (Vino Rosso di Montepulciano)

SERVES 4–6

PREPARATION 20 min

COOKING 75 min

DIFFICULTY level 1

Potato Soup
with pasta

If there are no fresh beans available, cook the other vegetables together and add one (14-oz/400-g) can of drained white kidney or cannellini beans with the pasta.

Place the potatoes, beans, tomato, leek, celery, sage, thyme, and parsley in a large saucepan with the oil and salt. Pour in the water and bring to a boil over low heat. Simmer for 45 minutes.

Set aside 1 cup of the cooked vegetables to garnish. Run the rest through a food mill or process in a food processor or blender. If it seems too dense, dilute with boiling water.

Return the soup to the saucepan, bring to a boil, add the pasta and cook until al dente. Stir in the reserved vegetables. Season with pepper and the Parmesan and serve hot.

1½ lb (750 g) waxy potatoes, peeled and cut into chunks

1 cup (100 g) fresh white beans, such as kidney or cannellini

1 firm-ripe tomato, peeled and chopped

White of 1 leek, finely chopped

1 stalk celery, finely chopped

2 leaves fresh sage, chopped

1 sprig thyme, chopped

1 small bunch fresh parsley, finely chopped

3 tablespoons extra-virgin olive oil

Salt

2 quarts (2 liters) water + extra boiling water as needed

8 oz (250 g) dried small soup pasta

Freshly ground black pepper

6 tablespoons freshly grated Parmesan cheese

Suggested wine: a dry red (Chianti Classico)

Spelt Soup

If using dried beans, soak them overnight in cold water, drain and rinse.

Cover the beans with cold water, add the garlic, sage, tomatoes (skins pierced with a fork), and a little salt (unless using dried beans). Cover and bring to a boil and simmer until tender, about 25 minutes (longer if dried beans are used, adding salt at the end).

Remove and discard the garlic and sage. Purée half the beans in a food mill, reserving the cooking liquid.

Heat the oil in a heavy-bottomed saucepan over medium heat and sauté the pancetta for 3 minutes with the crushed garlic. Discard the garlic as soon as it starts to color. Add the remaining vegetables and the tomato purée, salt, pepper, and stock. Stir well, cover, and simmer over low heat for 30 minutes before adding the drained spelt.

After another 20 minutes, add the two bean mixtures. Adjust the seasoning and simmer for a final 20 minutes.

Drizzle each portion with 1 tablespoon of oil and serve hot.

14 oz (400 g) fresh hulled (shelled) cannellini beans or 1 cup (200 g) dried cannellini beans

1 cup (200 g) quick-cooking spelt (or pearl barley)

2 cloves garlic, whole

1 small sprig sage

3 cherry tomatoes or small tomatoes

Salt and freshly ground black pepper

$1/3$ cup (90 ml) extra-virgin olive oil + extra for serving with the soup

4 oz (125 g) finely chopped pancetta

2 cloves garlic, lightly bruised

1 onion, very thinly sliced

1 leek, thinly sliced

1 stalk celery, thinly sliced

1 carrot, peeled and diced

5 oz (150 g) young spinach or Swiss chard (silverbeet) leaves, washed and shredded

$1/2$ small, dark green cabbage, washed and shredded

3 tablespoons tomato purée

$1 1/2$ quarts (1.5 liters) stock (homemade or bouillon cube)

Suggested wine: a young, dry red (Chianti Rufina)

Fish Soup

Soak the mussels and clams in cold water for 1 hour.

Drain well. Place in a frying pan over high heat and cook until they are all open. Discard any that have not opened. Set aside.

Half fill a medium pan with water, and add the onion, celery, carrot, parsley, basil, bay leaf, and 1 teaspoon of salt. Place over medium heat, cover, and bring to the boil. Add the hake, red mullet, and monkfish head and bring to the boil again. Lower the heat, partially cover the pan and cook for 20 minutes. Turn off the heat. Drain the stock through a colander into a tureen, discard the monkfish head, onion, celery, carrot, parsley, basil, and bay leaf.

Push the fish through a food mill and set aside in a bowl.

Pour the oil into a large frying pan and sauté the chopped garlic and parsley over medium heat for 5 minutes. Add the chile, squid, and octopus. Simmer for 10 minutes, or until reduced.

Pour in the wine and cook for 4 minutes. Lower the heat, add the diced tomatoes, stir, and check the seasoning. Cover and simmer over low heat for 20 minutes then add the creamed fish mixture, stock, the whole shrimp or saltwater crayfish, the smooth dogfish or shark and monkfish, its central bone removed, cut into four pieces, mussels, and clams. Simmer for 10 minutes.

Toast the bread and rub the slices with the clove of garlic. Place a piece of toast in each soup bowl and ladle the soup over the top. Serve hot.

14 oz (400 g) mussels, in shell
14 oz (400 g) clams, in shell
Salt
$1/2$ onion
1 stalk celery and 1 carrot,
    both cut in half
1 bunch parsley
5 basil leaves
1 bay leaf
8 oz (250 g) hake
8 oz (250 g) red mullet
8 oz (250 g) monkfish (with the head
    if possible)
$1/3$ cup (90 ml) extra-virgin olive oil
8 oz (250 g) octopus, cut into bite-sized
    pieces
8 oz (250 g) white fish fillets, cut into
    bite-sized pieces
8 oz (250 g) squid, cut into bite-sized
    pieces
6 cloves garlic, 5 finely chopped
    + 1 whole clove
$1/2$ cup finely chopped parsley
1 red chile, chopped
1 cup dry white wine
14 oz (400 g) plum tomatoes,
    peeled and diced
4 cups (1 liter) fish stock
4 medium shrimp or saltwater crayfish
8 oz (250 g) smooth dogfish or shark
6–8 slices firm-textured white bread

Wine: a dry white
    (Ansonica Costa dell'Argentario)

Tuscan Bread Soup

Plunge the tomatoes into a pan of boiling water for 1 minute, then into cold water. Peel and cut them in half horizontally. Squeeze gently to remove the seeds, then chop the flesh into small pieces.

Heat half the oil in a heavy-bottomed saucepan and sauté the garlic and bay leaves for 2–3 minutes. Add the bread and simmer over medium-low heat for 3–4 minutes, stirring frequently.

Stir in the tomatoes and, using a ladle, add about 2 cups of water. Season with salt and pepper. Simmer for 15 minutes, stirring often. If the soup becomes too thick, add a little more water (it should be about the same consistency as porridge).

Drizzle with the remaining oil, sprinkle with the basil, and serve.

2 lb (1 kg) firm ripe tomatoes
1/2 cup (125 ml) extra-virgin olive oil
3 cloves garlic, finely chopped
2 bay leaves
1 lb (500 g) firm-textured bread, 2 days old, cut in 1-inch cubes
Salt and freshly ground black pepper
8–10 fresh basil leaves, torn

Suggested wine: a light, dry red (Chianti dei Colli Aretini)

SEAFOOD

SERVES 4–6

PREPARATION 15 min + 1 h to marinate

COOKING 20 min

DIFFICULTY level 1

Spicy Sardines

Dredge the sardines in the flour, making sure they are well coated.

Heat the oil in a large frying pan over medium heat. Fry the sardines until golden brown, about 5 minutes on both sides. Drain well on paper towels and place in an earthenware dish.

In the same pan, sauté the garlic and red pepper flakes for 2–3 minutes. Pour in the vinegar and let it reduce. Add the bay leaf and rosemary. Season with salt and pepper. Pour in the water and bring to a boil. Simmer for 5 minutes.

Pour the sauce over the sardines and let marinate for at least 1 hour before serving.

24 large sardines, cleaned
$2/3$ cup (100 g) all-purpose (plain) flour
$1/2$ cup (125 ml) extra-virgin olive oil
5 cloves garlic, finely chopped
1 teaspoon red pepper flakes
1 tablespoon white wine vinegar
1 bay leaf
1 sprig rosemary
Salt and freshly ground black pepper
1 cup (250 ml) water

Suggested wine: a dry white
(Alcamo)

Sardine Rolls
sicilian style

Preheat the oven to 400°F (200°C/gas 6). Oil a baking dish. Use a sharp knife to remove the scales and heads from the sardines. Use kitchen scissors to slit them open along their bellies and remove the viscera and bones, then open them out flat. If preferred, ask your fish vendor to do this for you. Rinse carefully and dry with paper towels.

Heat half the oil in a large frying pan over medium heat and add two-thirds of the bread crumbs. Stir for 1–2 minutes, then set aside in a large bowl.

Place 1 tablespoon of oil and the anchovies in a small pan. Crush with a fork over low heat so that the anchovies turn into a paste. Stir the anchovies into the bread crumbs with the raisins, pine nuts, capers, olives, parsley, lemon juice and zest, sugar, a little salt, and a generous sprinkling of pepper. Mix well.

Lay the sardines out flat, skin-side downward, and spread some of the mixture on each.

Roll the sardines up, starting at the head end, and place in the prepared dish. Pack them closely together, tail downward, and wedge a bay leaf between each one. Sprinkle with the remaining bread crumbs and drizzle with the remaining oil.

Bake until tender, 20–25 minutes. Serve hot or at room temperature.

1½–1¾ lb (700–800 g) fresh large sardines
½ cup (125 ml) extra-virgin olive oil
1¾ cups (100 g) fresh bread crumbs
8–10 salt-cured anchovy fillets
3 tablespoons golden raisins (sultanas), soaked and drained
3 tablespoons pine nuts
1 tablespoon salt-cured capers
5 large black olives, pitted and chopped
1 tablespoon finely chopped parsley
1 tablespoon freshly squeezed lemon juice
Grated zest of ½ lemon
1 teaspoon sugar
Salt and freshly ground black pepper
Bay leaves

Suggested wine: a dry white
(Bianco di Donnafugata)

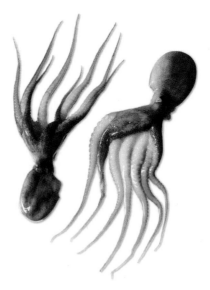

Fried Calamari
with almonds

Place the flour in a bowl and season with salt and pepper. Place the eggs in another bowl and the bread crumbs and almonds in third bowl.

Dredge the calamari in the flour, shaking off any excess. Dip in the egg and roll in the bread crumbs and almonds.

Heat the oil in a frying pan until very hot and fry the calamari in batches. Remove with a slotted spoon as they turn golden brown (about 5 minutes) and drain on paper towels. Do not cook for longer or they will become tough.

Garnish with the parsley and lemon and serve.

1/2 cup (75 g) all-purpose (plain) flour
Salt and freshly ground black pepper
2 eggs, beaten
1²/3 cups (250 g) fine dry bread crumbs
1/2 cup (50 g) almonds, finely chopped
1 quart (1 liter) olive oil, for frying
14 oz (400 g) calamari bodies,
      cut in 1/2-inch (5-mm) wide rings
Sprigs of parsley, to garnish
1 lemon, sliced, to garnish

Suggested wine: a dry white
      (Colli Euganei Bianco)

Fried Tuna Balls

Place the ricotta in a large bowl and mash well with a fork. Use the fork to mash the tuna, breaking it into flakes. Add to the bowl with the chopped parsley, Parmesan, salt, and egg. Mix until evenly blended.

Scoop up spoonfuls of the mixture with a dessert spoon and shape into balls about the size of a golf ball. Dredge in the flour.

Heat the oil in a large frying pan until very hot and fry in batches of 6–8, turning constantly, until golden brown, about 5 minutes each batch. Remove from the frying pan with a slotted spoon and drain on paper towels.

Garnish with the sprigs of parsley, season with extra salt, if liked, and serve immediately.

12 oz (350 g) fresh ricotta cheese, drained

10 oz (300 g) canned tuna, drained

2 tablespoons finely chopped parsley
    + sprigs to garnish

4 tablespoons freshly grated Parmesan
    cheese

Salt

1 egg

1/2 cup (75 g) all-purpose (plain) flour

2 cups (500 ml) olive oil, for frying

Suggested wine: a dry white
    (Greco di Bianco)

Stockfish Cream

SERVES 6

PREPARATION 10 min + 20 min to stand

COOKING 10 min

DIFFICULTY level 3

Place the stockfish in a large saucepan with enough cold water to cover over medium heat. Bring to a boil then turn off the heat. Let stand for 20 minutes then drain.

Remove the skin and all the bones. Break up into small pieces and transfer to a large bowl. Beat vigorously and continuously with a balloon whisk as you gradually add the oil in a steady trickle. Keep beating in the same direction and adding oil until the fish will absorb no more. The mixture should be light and fluffy like a mousse. Add a little more salt, if needed, and season generously with pepper.

Stir in the garlic and parsley. Serve at room temperature.

2 lb (1 kg) presoaked stockfish
1 cup (250 ml) extra-virgin olive oil
Salt and freshly ground black pepper
2 cloves garlic, finely chopped
2 tablespoons finely chopped parsley

Suggested wine: a dry white
    (Est! Est!! Est!!! di Montefiascone)

Baked Scallops

Preheat the oven to 350°F (180°C/gas 4).

If not already shucked, use a sharp knife to open the scallops. Extract the white mollusk and the pinky-red coral.

Rinse the scallops and coral carefully under cold running water and drain well. If you have scallop shells, place 16 half shells on a baking sheet and place a scallop and some coral in each one. (If you don't have shells, place the scallops in an ovenproof dish.) Sprinkle with the mushrooms, garlic, and parsley. Top with the bread crumbs and tomatoes, a few drops of lemon juice, and the oil. Season with salt.

Cook for 10 minutes. Moisten with the wine and cook for 3 more minutes. Serve hot.

16 fresh sea scallops, in shell (if possible)
8 small white mushrooms, finely chopped
4 cloves garlic, finely chopped
4 tablespoons finely chopped parsley
$1\frac{1}{2}$ cups (90 g) fresh bread crumbs
$\frac{1}{4}$ cup (60 g) peeled tomatoes, finely chopped
Freshly squeezed juice of $\frac{1}{2}$ lemon
2 tablespoons extra-virgin olive oil
Salt
$\frac{1}{2}$ cup (125 ml) dry white wine

Suggested wine: a dry white
   (Valle Venosta Chardonnay)

Seafood Fry

Cut the calamari bodies into rings and leave the tentacles whole. Do not shell the shrimp.

Place the flour in a large dish and dredge all the seafood in it, shaking off the excess.

Place the floured seafood on a large sheet of aluminum foil laid on a work surface or on a tray or platter.

Heat the oil in a deep fryer to very hot. Deep-fry the fish in batches until golden brown all over, about 5 minutes each batch.

Scoop out with a slotted spoon and drain on paper towels. Season with salt lightly and transfer to a serving plate.

Decorate with the wedges of lemon. Serve hot.

14 oz (450 g) calamari, cleaned
14 oz (450 g) shrimp
12 oz (350 g) baby cuttlefish
2 cups (300 g) all-purpose (plain) flour
1 quart (1 liter) olive oil, for frying
Salt
1 lemon, cut into wedges

Suggested wine: a dry white
    (Cinque Terre)

Roast Grouper
with potatoes

Preheat the oven to 400°F (200°C/gas 6).

Rinse the fish in cold running water and dry with paper towels.

Fill the cavity with the garlic, half the rosemary and sage, the salt, pepper, and lemon slices.

Peel the potatoes and cut into bite-sized chunks. Don't leave them too large, they must cook in the same time the fish takes to cook.

Pour half the oil into the bottom of a roasting pan and add the potatoes and the remaining rosemary and sage. Roll the potatoes in the oil.

Place the fish in the pan, making sure that it touches the bottom (not on the potatoes). Arrange the potatoes around the fish. Drizzle with the remaining oil and bake until the fish is cooked and the potatoes are browned and cooked through, 30 minutes. Turn the potatoes every 10 minutes during the roasting time and baste them and the fish with the oil, so that they brown evenly.

Place the fish on a serving platter with the potatoes and serve hot.

1 grouper, about 2½ lb (1.2 kg), gutted
2 cloves garlic, peeled and cut in half
¼ cup fresh rosemary leaves
6 sage leaves
Salt and freshly ground black pepper
1 lemon, thickly sliced
2 lb (1 kg) potatoes
¾ cup (200 ml) extra-virgin olive oil

Suggested wine: a dry white (Vermentino di Gallura)

Fried Swordfish
with herbs

Rinse the swordfish steaks and dry them carefully with paper towels.

Heat ¼ cup (60 ml) of oil in a large frying pan over high heat.

Dredge the swordfish steaks in the flour, shaking off any excess.

When the oil is hot, fry until golden brown, 5–7 minutes each side. Remove from the pan and drain on paper towels.

Mix the remaining oil with the garlic, parsley, oregano, thyme, and chile pepper in a small pan. Season with salt and pepper and simmer over medium heat for 10 minutes.

Pour the sauce over the swordfish steaks and serve hot.

6 swordfish steaks, about 8 oz
   (250 g) each
⅔ cup (180 ml) extra-virgin olive oil
½ cup (75 g) all-purpose (plain) flour
2 cloves garlic, finely chopped
¼ cup finely chopped parsley
1 tablespoon finely chopped fresh oregano
1 tablespoon finely chopped fresh thyme
1 dried chile pepper, crumbled
Salt and freshly ground black pepper

Suggested wine: a dry white
   (Bianco dell'Etna)

SERVES 6

PREPARATION 20 min

COOKING 35 min

DIFFICULTY level 1

Baked Plaice
with capers

Preheat the oven to 350°F (180°C/gas 4).

Rinse the fillets under cold running water and dry with paper towels.

Grease a large ovenproof dish with half the oil. Place the fillets in the dish and sprinkle with salt, pepper, capers, and the cherry tomatoes. Drizzle with the remaining oil.

Bake in a preheated until just tender, 10–15 minutes. Serve hot.

1¼ lb (600 g) plaice or flounder fillets
¼ cup (60 ml) extra-virgin olive oil
Salt and freshly ground white pepper
2 tablespoons salt-cured capers
16 cherry tomatoes, cut in half

Suggested wine: a dry white
    (Gavi di Gavi)

SERVES 4

PREPARATION 25 min

COOKING 25 min

DIFFICULTY level 2

Salt Cod
tuscan style

Cut the salt cod into 1½-inch (4-cm) pieces.

Place the flour on a plate and dredge the salt cod pieces in it, shaking off any excess.

Heat half the oil in a large frying pan over medium heat and fry the salt cod on both sides until golden, about 3 minutes each side. Remove from the pan, draining off the oil, and set aside.

Heat the remaining oil in the same pan. Sauté the garlic and parsley for 3 minutes, then add the tomatoes. Add the salt cod and season lightly with salt and pepper. Simmer for 15 minutes, turning the salt cod pieces carefully so as not to break them.

Serve hot.

2 lb (1 kg) salt cod, presoaked

1 cup (150 g) all-purpose (plain) flour

½ cup (125 ml) extra-virgin olive oil

2 cloves garlic, finely chopped

2 tablespoons finely chopped parsley

1 lb (500 g) plum tomatoes, peeled and chopped

Salt and freshly ground black pepper

Suggested wine: a dry white
(Vernaccia di San Gimignano)

SERVES 4

PREPARATION 15 min

COOKING 25 min

DIFFICULTY level 1

Smooth Hound

with pink peppercorns

Preheat the oven to 325°F (160°C/gas 3).

Place a large sheet of aluminum foil in a large baking dish, leaving the edges overhanging. There should be enough foil to fold over the dish containing the fish.

Lay the smooth hound steaks on the foil in the dish. Drizzle with the oil and sprinkle with the rosemary, chives, pink peppercorns, and salt. Fold the foil over the fish, sealing it well.

Bake for 25 minutes. Serve hot, straight from the package.

4 smooth hound steaks,
    about 1¼ lb (600 g) total weight
2 tablespoons extra-virgin olive oil
1 teaspoon finely chopped rosemary
1 teaspoon finely chopped chives
2 tablespoons pink peppercorns
Salt

Suggested wine: a dry white
    (Sylvaner della Valle Isarco)

POULTRY

Chicken Galantine
(cold stuffed chicken)

Combine the beef, pork, turkey, veal, and mortadella in a large bowl. Mix well and add the pistachios, egg, and truffle, if using. Season with salt and pepper and mix thoroughly.

Stuff the chicken with the mixture and sew up the neck and stomach cavity openings with a trussing needle and string. Use your hands to give the chicken a rectangular shape. Wrap in a piece of cheesecloth (muslin) and tie with kitchen string.

Place a large saucepan of salted water over medium heat. Add the onion, carrot, celery, parsley, peppercorns, and stock cube. When the water is boiling, carefully add the stuffed chicken and simmer over low heat for 1 hour 30 minutes.

Remove from the heat and drain the stock (which makes an excellent, light soup).

Carefully remove the cheesecloth and place the chicken between two trays, with a weight (for example, a brick) on top. This will help to eliminate any liquid absorbed by the meat during cooking and will give it a rectangular shape.

When cool transfer to the refrigerator, with the weight still on top, and chill for at least 12 hours.

In the meantime prepare the gelatin, following the directions on the package. Be sure to add the lemon juice while the gelatin is still liquid.

Serve the galantine thinly sliced on a serving dish, topped with the diced gelatin.

- 12 oz (300 g) lean ground (minced) beef
- 5 oz (150 g) lean ground (minced) pork
- 5 oz (150 g) ground (minced) turkey breast
- 5 oz (150 g) ground (minced) veal
- 2 oz (60 g) ground (minced) mortadella
- 1/2 cup (75 g) pistachios, shelled
- 1 egg
- 1 oz (30 g) black truffle, finely sliced (optional)
- Salt and freshly ground black pepper
- 1 chicken, boneless, about 4 lb (2 kg)
- 1 onion, cut in half
- 1 carrot, cut in 3
- 1 stalk celery, cut in 3
- 2 sprigs parsley
- 8 peppercorns
- 1 chicken stock cube
- 2 gelatin cubes
- Freshly squeezed juice of 1/2 lemon

Suggested wine: a light, dry white (Soave Classico)

Turkey Breast Roll

SERVES 4–6
PREPARATION 30 min
COOKING 1 h 15 min
DIFFICULTY level 2

Preheat the oven to 400°F (200°C/gas 6).

Use a sharp knife to open the turkey breast out to a rectangular shape. Beat lightly with a meat pounder, taking care not to tear the meat.

Melt the butter in a frying pan over medium heat. Add the the zucchini, carrot, and onion and sauté until the vegetables are softened, about 5 minutes. Season with salt and pepper and set aside to cool for a few minutes.

Season the turkey with salt and pepper, cover with the ham, and sprinkle with the vegetables. Roll the meat up and wrap with slices of pancetta. Truss with kitchen string, making two twists lengthwise as well, to fix the pancetta firmly to the turkey.

Place the meat in an ovenproof dish with the garlic, sage, and oil. Bake for 50 minutes, turning the meat during cooking and basting with the wine from time to time.

Remove from the oven and set the meat aside to cool. Discard the kitchen string; the meat will keep its shape when cool. Leave the oven on.

Roll the pastry out into a thin sheet on a lightly floured work surface. Wrap it round the meat, brush with the egg and decorate the top with pieces of leftover pastry.

Butter and flour a baking dish. Carefully place the roll in the dish, seam-side down. Bake until the pastry is golden brown, about 20 minutes.

Serve hot.

2½ lb (1.2 kg) turkey breast, in 1 piece
1 zucchini (courgette) and 1 carrot, sliced in julienne strips
1 onion, thinly sliced
2 tablespoons butter
Salt and freshly ground black pepper
4 oz (125 g) ham, cut in small cubes
6 oz (180 g) pancetta, thinly sliced
1 clove garlic, cut in half
4 leaves sage
⅓ cup (90 ml) extra-virgin olive oil
½ cup (125 ml) dry white wine
10 oz (300 g) frozen puff pastry, thawed
1 egg, beaten

Suggested wine: a dry white (Pinot Grigio)

Chicken Balls
with bell peppers and black olives

Cut the eggplant in thick slices, sprinkle with salt and place in a colander for 20 minutes. Cut into cubes.

Heat 1/4 cup (60 ml) of the oil in a large frying pan over medium heat. Sauté the garlic and onion until softened, 3–4 minutes. Add the peppers, eggplant, zucchini, tomatoes, and olives. Season with salt and pepper. Simmer for about 20 minutes, adding a little water if the pan becomes too dry.

In the meantime, combine the chicken, bread, Parmesan, egg, parsley, and a little salt in a bowl and mix thoroughly. Shape the mixture (which should be quite firm) into small round balls. Dredge in the flour.

Heat the remaining oil in a large frying pan over a medium heat and fry the balls until golden brown all over.

Add the vegetable mixture, season with salt and pepper, and simmer for 15 minutes, stirring carefully from time to time. If the dish dries out too much, add stock as required.

Transfer to a heated serving dish, sprinkle with the basil and serve hot.

1 eggplant (aubergine)
Salt and freshly ground black pepper
1/2 cup (125 ml) extra-virgin olive oil
1 clove garlic
1 large onion, thickly sliced
2 yellow bell peppers (capsicums), diced
1 zucchini (courgette), diced
10 cherry tomatoes, cut in half
1/2 cup (50 g) black olives
1 1/2 lb (600 g) ground (minced) chicken breast
2 tablespoons crustless bread, soaked in milk and squeezed
1/2 cup (60 g) freshly grated Parmesan cheese
1 egg
1 tablespoon parsley, finely chopped
1/2 cup (75 g) all-purpose (plain) flour
1/2 cup (125 ml) beef stock (homemade or bouillon cube)
10 leaves basil, torn

Wine: a dry, fruity white (Verdicchio)

SERVES 4

PREPARATION 10 min

COOKING 45 min

DIFFICULTY level 1

Braised Chicken
with bell peppers

Rinse the chicken under cold running water and dry with paper towels. Cut into 8 pieces.

Sauté the garlic in 2 tablespoons of oil for 2–3 minutes, then add the tomatoes. Season with salt and pepper and simmer over medium-low heat until the sauce reduces, about 15 minutes.

Clean the bell peppers, removing the seeds and core. Cut in quarters and place under the broiler (grill) until the skin blackens. Peel the blackened skin away with your fingers. Rinse the peppers and dry with paper towels. Cut into thin strips.

Sauté the chicken in the remaining oil. Season with salt and pepper, then pour in the wine. Simmer over medium-low heat for 15 minutes.

Add the tomato sauce and bell peppers and simmer until the chicken is cooked through, about 10 minutes. Serve hot.

1 chicken, about 3 lb (1.5 kg) lb
3 cloves garlic, finely chopped
1/2 cup (125 ml) extra-virgin olive oil
14 oz (400 g) peeled and chopped canned or fresh tomatoes
Salt and freshly ground black pepper
1 lb (500 g) bell peppers, mixed colors
1 cup (250 ml) dry white wine

Suggested wine: a light, dry red (Velletri Rosso)

Braised Chicken
with black olives

Rinse the chicken under cold running water. Dry well and cut into 8 pieces.

Heat the butter and garlic in a large frying pan over medium heat. Remove the garlic when lightly browned. Add the chicken pieces and sauté until golden brown all over.

Season with salt and pepper and pour in the wine and vinegar. Simmer until the liquids have almost evaporated. Add the olives and anchovies, if using, partially cover the frying pan, and simmer over low heat until the chicken is tender, about 40 minutes.

Transfer to a heated serving dish and serve hot.

1 chicken, about 3 lb (1.5 kg)
$1/4$ cup (60 g) butter
2 cloves garlic, peeled and lightly crushed
Salt and freshly ground black pepper
$1/2$ cup (125 ml) dry white wine
2 tablespoons white wine vinegar
100 g black olives, pitted and chopped
6 anchovy fillets (optional)

Suggested wine: a dry white
    (Orvieto Classico)

Fried Chicken

Place the chicken in a large bowl and sprinkle with the parsley. Add the lemon juice and olive oil. Season with salt and pepper. Cover and let marinate for 2 hours.

Beat the eggs until frothy in a medium bowl. Place the flour in a bowl.

Heat the sunflower oil to very hot in a deep frying pan or deep fryer over medium heat. Drain the chicken from the marinade. Dredge in the flour, ensuring that it is evenly coated. Shake to remove any excess flour. Dip each piece of chicken in the beaten egg.

Fry in two batches in the hot oil until cooked through and golden brown, about 15 minutes each batch. Drain on paper towels. Serve hot.

3 lb (1.5 kg) chicken thighs
3 tablespoons finely chopped parsley
Freshly squeezed juice of 1 large lemon
5 tablespoons extra-virgin olive oil
Salt and freshly ground black pepper
2 large eggs
1/2 cup (75 g) all-purpose (plain) flour
2 cups (500 ml) sunflower oil, for frying

Suggested wine: a full-bodied dry red
    (Vino Nobile di Montepulciano)

Chicken Breast
with lemon and cognac

Place the flour on a plate. Dredge the chicken in the flour, ensuring that each piece is evenly coated. Shake gently to remove any excess flour.

Melt half the butter in a large frying pan over medium-high heat. Add the prosciutto and sauté until crisp, about 2 minutes. Add the chicken in a single layer (make sure the pieces don't overlap). Sauté until browned on both sides, about 5 minutes.

Add the wine and cognac and cook until evaporated, 4–5 minutes. Add the parsley and lemon juice. Dust with cayenne pepper and season with salt. Simmer until the meat is cooked through, about 2 minutes. Transfer to a heated serving dish.

Remove the pan from the heat and add the remaining butter. Let the butter melt and mix well. Drizzle the sauce over the chicken. Serve hot.

- 1/2 cup (75 g) all-purpose (plain) flour
- 2 boneless skinless chicken breasts, thinly sliced
- 1/3 cup (90 g) butter
- 2 oz (60 g) prosciutto, finely chopped
- 1/3 cup (90 ml) dry white wine
- 2 tablespoons cognac
- 4 tablespoons finely chopped parsley
- Freshly squeezed juice of 1 lemon
- Pinch cayenne pepper
- Salt

Suggested wine: a dry red
(Sangiovese di Romagna)

Turkey Breast
in cream of onion sauce

Roll the turkey breast and tie with kitchen string. Season with salt and pepper and roll in the flour.

Place in a heavy-bottomed pan with the oil and butter and sauté over high heat for 5–7 minutes. Add the onions, stirring carefully and making sure the turkey is always touching the bottom of the pan (rather than on the onions). Sauté for 5 minutes more.

Pour in enough stock to almost cover the meat. Partially cover the pan and lower the heat to medium-low. Add more stock during cooking, as required. When cooked, the turkey will be light brown and the onions will have melted to form a delicious, creamy sauce, about 50 minutes.

Slice and arrange on a serving dish. Smother with the onion sauce.

2½ lb (1.2 kg) turkey breast
Salt and freshly ground black pepper
3 tablespoons all-purpose (plain) flour
½ cup (125 ml) extra-virgin olive oil
1 tablespoon butter
4 large white onions, coarsely sliced
1 quart (1 liter) beef stock
   (homemade or bouillon cube)

Suggested wine: a dry red
   (Donnaz)

SERVES 4

PREPARATION 15 min

COOKING 50 min

DIFFICULTY level 1

Chicken Patties
with lentils

Fill a large saucepan with water and bring to a boil. Add the lentils and cook until tender, about 30 minutes.

Drain the lentils and transfer to a bowl with the remaining ingredients (except the oil), and mix well. Shape into 8 patties.

Heat the oil in a large frying pan to very hot. Fry the patties until golden brown on both sides, 8–10 minutes.

Drain on paper towels and serve hot.

¾ cup (100 g) red lentils
12 oz (350 g) ground (minced) cooked chicken
1 cup (120 g) fine dry bread crumbs
1 tablespoon lemon juice
1 teaspoon finely chopped oregano
Salt and freshly ground black pepper
2 cups (500 ml) oil, for frying

Suggested wine: a smooth dry red (Aprilia Merlot)

Chicken Stew

Sauté the onion and garlic in the oil in a large frying pan until pale gold. Add the chicken and brown all over.

Pour in the wine and simmer until it evaporates. Add the potatoes, carrots, celery, and parsley and season with salt and pepper. Pour in enough stock to moisten the dish, cover and simmer over low heat for 30–35 minutes, stirring frequently. Add more stock as required during cooking.

When the chicken is cooked and the vegetables are tender, remove from heat and serve hot.

1 large onion, finely chopped
2 cloves garlic, finely chopped
1/4 cup (60 ml) extra-virgin olive oil
1 chicken, 3 lb (1.5 kg), cut into 8 pieces
1/2 cup (125 ml) dry white wine
14 oz (400 g) potatoes, coarsely chopped
4 medium carrots, coarsely chopped
2 stalks celery, coarsely chopped
2 tablespoons finely chopped parsley
Salt and freshly ground black pepper
2/3 cup (150 ml) chicken stock
      (homemade or bouillon cube)

Suggested wine: a dry red
      (Rosso Piceno)

SERVES 4

PREPARATION 15 min

COOKING 20 min

DIFFICULTY level 1

Turkey Breast
with olives and sundried tomatoes

Cut the turkey into thin strips about 3 inches (8 cm) long.

Sauté the shallots with the chile pepper in the oil in a large frying pan over medium heat for 5 minutes.

Add the turkey and sauté over high heat for 3 minutes. Season with salt and pepper. Add the olives and tomatoes. Drizzle with the wine and let it evaporate. Add the stock and rosemary. Simmer over low heat until the turkey is cooked, 5–10 minutes.

Serve hot.

1 lb (500 g) turkey breast

2 shallots, coarsely chopped

1 fresh red chile pepper, finely sliced

2 tablespoons extra-virgin olive oil

Salt and freshly ground black pepper

15 green olives, pitted

10 black olives, pitted and coarsely chopped

5 sundried tomatoes, coarsely chopped

1/4 cup (60 ml) dry white wine

1/4 cup (60 ml) chicken stock (homemade or bouillon cube)

1 sprig rosemary

Suggested wine: a full-bodied dry red (Vino Rosso di Montepulciano)

Turkey Bake
in tomato sauce

Preheat the oven to 400°F (200°C/gas 6).

Mix the turkey, sausage, pancetta, Parmesan, egg and egg yolk, bread crumbs, nutmeg, salt, and pepper in a large bowl.

Parboil the cabbage leaves in a large pan of salted water for 4 minutes. Drain well and dry with paper towels.

Arrange the cabbage leaves on a work surface in a rectangle; they should be overlapping so that there is no space between the leaves. Place the turkey mixture in the center of the leaves and shape into a loaf. Wrap the cabbage leaves around the loaf, taking care not to tear them. Tie with kitchen string.

Transfer to a baking dish. Mix the onion, tomatoes, and oil in a medium bowl and pour over the top.

Bake, basting often with the wine and stock, until the turkey is cooked through, about 1 hour 15 minutes. Slice and serve hot.

1¼ lb (600 g) ground (minced) turkey breast

8 oz (250 g) Italian pork sausage, skinned and crumbled

¼ cup (30 g) diced pancetta

1 cup (125 g) freshly grated Parmesan cheese

1 egg + 1 egg yolk

1 cup (60 g) fresh bread crumbs

⅛ teaspoon nutmeg

Salt and freshly ground black pepper

10 leaves Savoy cabbage

1 small onion, finely chopped

14 oz (400 g) peeled and chopped tomatoes

½ cup (125 ml) extra-virgin olive oil

½ cup (125 ml) dry white wine

½ cup (125 ml) beef stock (homemade or bouillon cube)

Suggested wine: a dry red (Chianti Riserva)

Hunter's Chicken

SERVES 4–6

PREPARATION 20 min

COOKING 1 h

DIFFICULTY level 1

Rinse the chicken inside and out under cold running water. Cut into 8–12 small pieces, leaving it on the bone. Pat dry with paper towels.

Sauté the onion in the oil in a large frying pan until pale golden brown. Remove the onion from the pan and set aside.

Add the pancetta to the flavored oil, followed by the chicken pieces. Simmer over a slightly higher heat for about 10 minutes, turning frequently.

Pour in the wine and cook until it evaporates. Add the tomatoes and the reserved onion. Season with salt and pepper. Cook until the chicken is very tender, about 30 minutes, stirring and turning at intervals. Serve hot.

1 chicken, about 3 lb (1.5 kg), cleaned
1 medium onion, thinly sliced
1/2 cup (125 ml) extra-virgin olive oil
3 oz (90 g) pancetta, chopped
1 cup (250 ml) dry white wine
8 oz (250 g) ripe tomatoes, blanched, peeled and diced
Salt and freshly ground black pepper

Suggested wine: a dry red (Assisi Rosso)

Chicken
with fennel seeds

Preheat the oven to 350°F (180°C/gas 4). Wash the chicken inside and out and dry with paper towels.

Mix the pancetta, garlic, sage, rosemary, parsley, fennel seeds, salt, and pepper in a small bowl and place in the cavity. Use a trussing needle and thread to sew up the opening.

Pour half the olive oil into a roasting pan, place the chicken in it and drizzle with the remaining oil. Season with salt and pepper.

Roast until the chicken is very tender, about 1 hour. Serve hot.

1 chicken, about 3 lb (1.5 kg), cleaned
3 oz (90 g) pancetta, finely chopped
2 cloves garlic, finely chopped
1 heaped teaspoon each, finely chopped fresh sage and rosemary
1 tablespoon finely chopped parsley
1 level teaspoon fennel seeds
1/3 cup (90 ml) extra-virgin olive oil
Salt and freshly ground black pepper

Suggested wine: a full-bodied dry red (Chianti Classico)

Roast Duck
with sausage stuffing

Preheat the oven to 350°F (180°C/gas 4).

Mix the sausage meat, liver, Parmesan, egg, and parsley in a large bowl. Season with salt and pepper. Shape into a large oval which will fit into the duck's cavity and coat it with the bread crumbs.

Season the duck inside and out with salt and pepper and place the rissole of stuffing in the cavity. Use a trussing needle and kitchen thread to sew up the bird. Truss the duck by tying the legs to its sides neatly with kitchen string. Dot the surface of the duck with the pork fat and rosemary.

Transfer to a roasting pan or ovenproof dish with the oil, butter, and sage. Roast until the duck is tender, about 1 hour 45 minutes.

Cut the duck into at least 6 portions and slice the stuffing. Arrange on a serving dish, spoon some of its cooking juices over the top, and serve.

¼ cup (60 g) Italian sausage meat, crumbled
½ cup (100 g) finely chopped duck liver
½ cup (60 g) freshly grated Parmesan cheese
1 egg
2 tablespoons finely chopped parsley
Salt and freshly ground black pepper
1 duck, about 4 lb (2 kg), cleaned
½ cup (60 g) fine dry bread crumbs
2 tablespoons finely chopped pork fat
1 sprig rosemary
5 tablespoons extra-virgin olive oil
¼ cup (60 g) butter
2 leaves sage

Suggested wine: a dry red (Grignolino)

Roast Duck
with orange

Preheat the oven to 375°F (190°C/gas 5). Wash and dry the duck and place the garlic, rosemary, salt, pepper, and the zest of 1 orange into the cavity.

Pour half the oil into a large roasting pan. Add the duck and season with more pepper. Arrange the onion, carrot, and celery around the duck and drizzle with the remaining oil. Roast for 10 minutes.

Pour the wine over the duck and roast for 1 hour and 20 minutes.

Peel the zest off the remaining 2 oranges and cut it into very thin strips. Place the zest in a small saucepan with cold water and bring to a boil. Drain. Repeat the process twice to remove any bitterness.

Heat the sugar, water, and lemon juice in a small saucepan over medium heat until the sugar melts and caramelizes. Add the strips of orange zest and stir over low heat for 2 minutes. Set aside.

Thirty minutes into the roasting time, squeeze the juice from 2 oranges over the duck.

When the duck is done (test by inserting a sharp knife into the thigh, if the juices run clear the duck is ready), remove the garlic, rosemary, and orange zest from the cavity.

Transfer the duck to a casserole with the cooking juices and vegetables and spoon the caramelized orange zest over the top. Simmer over medium heat for 5 minutes, turning the duck carefully. Serve hot.

1 duck, about 3 lb (1.5 kg), cleaned
2 cloves garlic, whole
Sprig of rosemary
Salt and freshly ground black pepper
3 oranges
5 tablespoons extra-virgin olive oil
1 onion, coarsely chopped
1 carrot, coarsely chopped
1 stalk celery, coarsely chopped
1/2 cup (125 ml) dry white wine
1/2 cup (100 g) sugar
1 1/2 tablespoons water
1 tablespoon freshly squeezed lemon juice

Suggested wine: a full-bodied dry red (Brunello)

MEAT

SERVES 4

PREPARATION 10 min

COOKING 20 min

DIFFICULTY level 1

Sliced Sirloin
with arugula

Wash and dry the arugula, chop coarsely, and set aside.

Heat 1 tablespoon of oil in a large frying pan over medium-high heat. Cook the slices of beef, 2–3 at a time, by dropping them into the pan and turning them immediately. They will only take a minute or two to cook.

When all the steak is cooked, arrange on a heated serving dish, season with salt and pepper, and cover with the arugula. Drizzle with the oil and lemon juice and serve immediately.

Variations: Replace the lemon juice with ¼ cup (60 ml) of balsamic vinegar. Add 10–12 cherry tomatoes, cut in half.

14 oz (400 g) sirloin, thinly sliced
2 bunches arugula (rocket)
Salt and freshly ground black pepper
Freshly squeezed juice of ½ lemon
¼ cup (60 ml) extra-virgin olive oil

Suggested wine: a dry, aromatic white
(Müller Thurgau)

Veal Scaloppine
with marsala and butter sauce

Remove any small pieces of fat from the scaloppine. Pound the meat lightly, dredge in the flour, and shake thoroughly.

Melt half the butter in a large frying pan over medium heat. Add the veal in a single layer, making sure that the pieces do not overlap. Cook until lightly browned, about 2 minutes on each side.

Add the Marsala and simmer for 3 minutes. Season with salt and pepper.

Place the meat on a heated serving dish. Remove the pan from the heat and add the remaining butter. Let the butter melt and mix well. Drizzle over the meat and serve hot.

8 veal scaloppine (escalopes), about 14 oz (400 g)
1/3 cup (50 g) all-purpose (plain) flour
1/3 cup (90 g) butter
1/3 cup (90 ml) dry Marsala wine
Salt and freshly ground black pepper

Suggested wine: a young, dry red (Barbaresco Giovane)

SERVES 4

PREPARATION 15 min

COOKING 15 min

DIFFICULTY level 1

Veal Scaloppine
with prosciutto and sage

Remove any small pieces of fat from the scaloppine. Pound the meat lightly, dredge in the flour, and shake thoroughly.

Place a slice of prosciutto on each scaloppine and top with a sage leaf. Use a toothpick to fix the prosciutto and sage to the slice of veal.

Melt the butter and oil in a large frying pan over medium heat. Add the scaloppine with the prosciutto facing downward. Brown over high heat, 2–3 minutes each side.

Season with salt and pepper. Pour in the wine and simmer until it evaporates, 3–4 minutes. Serve hot.

8 veal scaloppine (escalopes), about
    14 oz (400 g)
1/3 cup (50 g) all-purpose (plain) flour
4 oz (125 g) thinly sliced prosciutto
8 leaves sage
2 tablespoons butter
3 tablespoons extra-virgin olive oil
Salt and freshly ground black pepper
1/2 cup (125 ml) dry white wine

Wine: a light, dry rosé
    (Colli della Sabina)

SERVES 4

PREPARATION 20 min

COOKING 10 min

DIFFICULTY level 1

Veal Cutlets
with anchovy sauce

Pound the veal lightly. Make little cuts around the edges to stop them from curling during cooking.

Dredge the cutlets in the flour, shaking off any excess.

Beat the eggs in a bowl with the salt. Dip the cutlets in the egg, then coat with bread crumbs, pressing so they stick.

Heat the oil in a large frying pan until very hot and fry the cutlets until golden brown on both sides, 4–5 minutes each side. Drain on paper towels.

Prepare the anchovy sauce by melting the butter in a small saucepan over low heat. Stir in the anchovies, crushing them with a fork until they dissolve. When smooth, spoon over the cutlets. Serve hot.

4–8 veal cutlets, about 1 lb (500 g) total weight
2 eggs
Salt
1/2 cup (75 g) all-purpose (plain) flour
1 1/2 cups (250 g) fine dry bread crumbs
1/2 cup (125 ml) olive oil, for frying
1/2 cup (125 g) butter
8 anchovy fillets

Suggested wine: a dry rosé (Rosato di Leverano)

Boiled Beef
with onions

Place the beef in a large saucepan with cold water to cover. Add the onion, carrot, celery, parsley, whole tomatoes, and sea salt and bring slowly to a boil. Simmer over low heat until the beef is very tender, at least 1 hour. Remove the meat from the pan, reserving the stock (which can be frozen for later use).

Sauté the onions in the oil in a large saucepan over medium heat for 2–3 minutes. Pour in ½ cup (125 ml) of stock from the pan. Simmer until reduced, about 10 minutes.

Chop the beef into thin slices. Add to the onions, season with salt and pepper, and stir for 3–4 minutes. Stir in the canned tomatoes and season with salt. Cover and simmer over low heat for 15 minutes, adding more stock as required. Serve hot.

1½ lb (750 g) beef (brisket, rump roast, or bottom round/topside)
1 onion, cut in half
1 carrot, cut in 3–4 pieces
1 stalk celery, cut in 3–4 pieces
1 sprig parsley
2 tomatoes
1 tablespoon coarse sea salt
5 large onions, sliced
¼ cup (60 ml) extra-virgin olive oil
Salt and freshly ground black pepper
1 (14-oz/400-g) can tomatoes, with juice

Suggested wine: a smooth, dry red (Aprilia Merlot)

Beef Stew
with potatoes

Heat the oil in a large, heavy-bottomed pan. Add the garlic, onion, carrot, celery, tomatoes, and mixed herbs and sauté for 5 minutes.

Trim off any small pieces of fat from the meat. Add to the pan, season with salt and pepper, and sauté until brown, about 5 minutes.

Pour in the wine and simmer until it evaporates. Cover the pan and simmer over low heat for 1 hour, gradually adding the stock. Stir frequently, to stop the meat from sticking to the pan.

Add the potatoes and simmer until tender, about 30 minutes. Serve hot.

- 1/3 cup (90 ml) extra-virgin olive oil
- 1 clove garlic, 1 onion, 1 carrot, 1 stalk celery, all finely chopped
- 4 large tomatoes, peeled and chopped
- 1 tablespoon finely chopped, mixed herbs (sage, parsley, oregano, rosemary, thyme, etc)
- 1 1/2 lb (750 g) beef chuck with muscle, cut into bite-sized pieces
- Salt and freshly ground black pepper
- 1 cup (250 ml) dry red wine
- 2 cups (500 ml) beef stock (homemade or bouillon cube)
- 1 1/4 lb (600 g) potatoes, peeled and cut into bite-sized chunks

Suggested wine: a robust, dry red (Carmignano Rosso)

Boiled Meats

Place 1 onion, 2 stalks celery, 2 carrots, 15 peppercorns and 2 tablespoons of sea salt in a large pot of boiling water. Add the beef and when the water has returned to a boil, reduce the heat a little and cover. Simmer for 1 hour, then add the veal and chicken.

Simmer for 2 more hours, topping up with boiling water if necessary. Test the meats with a thin skewer: if they are not very tender, simmer for 30 more minutes or longer.

Meanwhile, in a separate pot, cook the calf's tongue with the remaining onion, celery, carrot, peppercorns, and sea salt. This will take about 2 hours. Time it so that it is ready at the same time as the other meats.

Place the cotechino sausage in a saucepan with enough cold water to cover. Bring to a boil over very low heat and simmer gently for the time indicated on the package.

Ideally, all the meats should be ready at the same time, but they will not spoil if kept in their cooking liquid until everything is done.

Slice the cotechino sausage, but leave the other meats whole. Arrange on heated serving platters. Serve hot or at room temperature.

2 medium onions, peeled, stuck with 4–6 cloves

3 stalks celery, trimmed and washed

3 medium carrots, peeled

20 black peppercorns

3 tablespoons coarse salt

3 lb (1.5 kg) boneless beef cuts from brisket, bottom round, or rump roast

2 lb (1 kg) boneless veal cuts, from breast or shoulder

1/2 large chicken

1 1/4 lb (600 g) calf's tongue

1 cotechino sausage, about 1 1/2 lb (750 g)

Suggested wine: a full-bodied, dry red (Barolo)

Roast Veal Roll

Preheat the oven to 375°F (190°C/gas 5).

Flatten the meat lightly with a meat pounder. Trim it to make a rough rectangle. Arrange the trimmings on top of the meat. Cover with a layer of the ham.

Beat the eggs in a large bowl. Add the parsley and milk. Season with salt and pepper.

Heat half the oil in a large frying pan over medium heat. Pour the egg mixture into the pan and cook until almost set, about 3 minutes. Slide onto a plate, flip onto another plate, and slide it back into the pan. Cook until the egg is set.

Lay the cooked egg frittata over the meat. Trim off any excess and place the trimmings on top.

Roll up the veal to make a roulade. Secure it with kitchen string. Tuck the rosemary and sage under the string. Season with salt and place in a roasting pan. Dot with the butter and drizzle with the remaining oil. Drizzle with the wine.

Roast until the meat is tender, 2–3 hours. Baste the meat from time to time while it is cooking and add a little more wine if it begins to dry out.

Place on a cutting board. Remove and discard the string, rosemary, and sage. Slice the meat and transfer it to a serving dish. Serve with the boiled vegetables.

1 lb (500 g) slice of veal
5 oz (150 g) ham, in large thick slices
2 eggs
1 cup (50 g) finely chopped parsley
2 tablespoons milk
Salt and freshly ground black pepper
1/3 cup (90 ml) extra-virgin olive oil
1 sprig rosemary
1 sprig sage
1/4 cup (60 g) butter
1/3 cup (90 ml) dry white wine
   + extra, as required
Boiled potatoes, carrots, and zucchini
   (courgettes), to serve

Suggested wine: a dry, aromatic white
   (Traminer Aromatico dell'Alto Adige)

Meat Loaf
with mushrooms

Preheat the oven to 350°F (180°C/gas 4).

Soak the bread in the milk for 5 minutes. Squeeze well and place in a large bowl. Add the veal, eggs, pecorino, ham, salt and pepper.

Mix well and shape the mixture into a meat loaf. Roll carefully first in the bread crumbs and then in the flour.

Heat the oil in a large saucepan over medium heat and brown the loaf on all sides. Pour in the wine and simmer for 5 minutes. Add the tomatoes, mushrooms, garlic, and parsley. Stir gently and transfer to an ovenproof dish or roasting pan.

Bake until the meat is cooked through, about 45 minutes.

Serve hot or at room temperature.

6 oz (180 g) white bread, crusts removed

2 cups (500 ml) milk

$1\frac{1}{4}$ lb (600 g) lean ground (minced) veal

2 eggs

$\frac{1}{4}$ cup (30 g) freshly grated pecorino cheese

2 oz (60 g) prosciutto, finely chopped

Salt and freshly ground black pepper

2 tablespoons fine dry bread crumbs

2 tablespoons all-purpose (plain) flour

$\frac{1}{4}$ cup (60 ml) extra-virgin oil

$\frac{1}{2}$ cup (125 ml) dry white wine

4 large ripe tomatoes, peeled and chopped

8 oz (250 g) white mushrooms, cleaned and coarsely copped

1 clove garlic, finely chopped

2 tablespoons parsley, finely chopped

Suggested wine: a light, dry red (Bardolino)

Tuscan Beef Stew

Dredge the meat in the flour, shaking off the excess.

Heat the oil in in a heavy-bottomed saucepan. Sauté the garlic, sage, and rosemary 3–4 minutes. Add the meat and brown all over, 5–7 minutes.

Add the tomatoes and season with salt and pepper and sauté for 5 minutes. Pour in the wine, cover, and simmer over low heat until the beef is very tender, about 2 hours. Add the stock gradually during cooking to keep the stew moist.

Serve hot.

2 lb (1 kg) beef chuck, round or shin, cut into bite-size pieces

½ cup (75 g) all-purpose (plain) flour

2 cloves garlic, finely chopped

1 tablespoon finely chopped sage

1 tablespoon finely chopped rosemary

5 tablespoons extra-virgin olive oil

1 (14-oz/400-g) can tomatoes, with juice

Salt and freshly ground black pepper

1 cup (250 ml) dry red wine

1 cup (250 ml) beef stock (homemade or bouillon cube)

Suggested wine: a full-bodied, dry red (Vino Nobile di Montepulciano)

Hot Tuscan Stew

SERVES 6

PREPARATION 10 min

COOKING 3 h

DIFFICULTY level 1

Place the meat in a large heavy-based saucepan with the garlic, tomatoes, salt, and pepper and add just enough of the water to cover the meat.

Partially cover the pan and simmer over low heat for 2 hours, adding extra water if the sauce becomes too dry. Stir from time to time.

After 2 hours, pour in the wine and simmer until the meat is very tender, about 1 hour.

Serve hot.

1½ lb (1.75 kg) muscle from veal shanks, cut in bite-sized pieces

4 cloves garlic, finely chopped

1¼ lb (600 g) tomatoes, peeled and chopped

Salt

4 tablespoons freshly ground black pepper

About 1 quart (1 liter) cold water

3 cups (750 ml) dry red wine

Suggested wine: a full-bodied, dry red (Chianti Classico Riserva)

Ossobuco
(braised veal shanks)

Dredge the meat in the flour. Shake gently to remove any excess.

Melt the butter in a large Dutch oven or heavy saucepan over medium heat. The pan should be large enough to hold the meat in a single layer. Add 1 clove of garlic, lightly crushed but whole. Sauté until pale golden brown, 3–4 minutes. Discard the garlic.

Add the meat and sauté until lightly browned, 3–4 minutes each side. Lower the heat and add half the wine. Simmer until the wine has evaporated, about 5 minutes. Add the remaining wine and simmer for 5 minutes. Add the nutmeg and season with salt and pepper. Simmer over low heat, adding a little stock from time to time, until the meat begins to come away from the bone, about 1 hour 30 minutes.

Place the remaining garlic, parsley, and lemon zest into a mortar and pestle and crush to make a coarse paste. Add a little rosemary or some anchovy paste to this mixture if liked. Add the paste to the pan and mix well. Simmer for 5 minutes then serve hot.

6 marrow bone steaks
1/2 cup (75 g) all-purpose (plain) flour
1/3 cup (90 g) butter
2 cloves garlic
1/3 cup (90 ml) dry white wine
Pinch of freshly grated nutmeg
Salt and freshly ground black pepper
2 cups (500 ml) beef stock
    (homemade or bouillon cube)
4 tablespoons finely chopped parsley
Freshly grated zest of 1 lemon
Leaves from 1 sprig of rosemary (optional)
1 tablespoon anchovy paste (optional)

Suggested wine: a smooth, dry white
    (Terlano Sauvignon)

Roast Spare Ribs

Preheat the oven to 350°F (180°C/gas 4).

Place the spare ribs in a large roasting pan. Season with salt and pepper, sprinkle with the rosemary, and drizzle with the oil. Use a sharp knife to make 8 incisions in the meaty parts of the spare ribs and fill each one with a piece of garlic.

Roast the spare ribs until tender and cooked through, 45–50 minutes. The exact cooking time will depend on how much meat is on the spare ribs. Serve hot.

5 lb (2.5 kg) spare pork ribs
Salt and freshly ground black pepper
2 tablespoons fresh rosemary leaves
$1/4$ cup (60 ml) extra-virgin olive oil
4 cloves garlic, peeled and cut in half

Wine: a dry, full-bodied red
    (Chianti Classico Riserva)

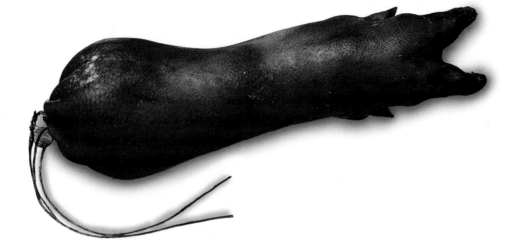

Zampone Sausage
with potatoes

Zampone are available prepackaged. Cook the sausage following the instructions on the package.

About 30 minutes before the sausage is cooked, boil the potatoes in a large pot of salted water until tender, about 25 minutes.

Mash the potatoes and stir in the milk and butter. Season with nutmeg, salt, and pepper.

Slice the cooked sausage and serve on a heated serving dish with the potatoes.

1 zampone, about 2 lb (1 kg)
1½ lb (750 g) potatoes, peeled
½ cup (125 ml) milk
1 tablespoon butter
Salt and freshly ground black pepper
Pinch of nutmeg

Suggested wine: a dry red
    (Pinot Nero dei Colli Piacentini)

Roast Lamb
with rosemary and garlic

Preheat the oven to 350°F (180°C/gas 4).

Place the lamb in an ovenproof dish large enough to hold it and the potatoes. Use the point of a sharp knife to make small incisions in the meat and push the pieces of garlic in. Close the meat around it, so that its flavor will permeate the meat during cooking. Sprinkle with the rosemary. Drizzle with the oil. Season with salt and pepper.

Place in the oven and begin roasting.

Peel the potatoes and cut into large bite-sized chunks. Arrange them around the meat after it has been in the oven for about 20 minutes. The meat should take about 1 hour to cook, while the potatoes will need only about 40 minutes. Baste the meat with the cooking juices 2 or 3 times during roasting and turn the potatoes so that they are evenly browned.

Serve hot.

Shoulder of baby lamb (with some
   loin attached), about 3 lb (1.5 kg)
3 cloves garlic, peeled and cut in half
4–6 sprigs fresh rosemary
½ cup (125 ml) extra-virgin olive oil
Salt and freshly ground black pepper
2 lb (1 kg) roasting potatoes,
   cut into large chunks

Wine: a dry red (Cerveteri Rosso)

VEGETABLES & SALADS

Mushrooms
baked with parmesan stuffing

Preheat the oven to 350°F (180°/gas 4).

Detach the stems from the mushrooms. Rinse the caps and stems under cold running water and dry with kitchen towel. Leave the caps whole. Chop the stems finely.

Place the stems in a bowl with the garlic, bread, salt and pepper and mix well. Add the eggs, Parmesan, oregano, parsley, marjoram, and 1 tablespoon of oil. Mix well.

Use this mixture to stuff the mushrooms, pressing it in carefully with your fingertips.

Oil an ovenproof dish just large enough to hold the mushrooms snugly. Fill with the mushrooms and drizzle with the remaining oil. Bake until tender, about 30 minutes.

Serve hot or at room temperature.

12 fresh medium mushrooms
1 small clove garlic, finely chopped
2 thick slices white bread, crusts removed, soaked in warm milk and gently squeezed dry
Salt and freshly ground black pepper
1 whole egg + 1 egg yolk
1⅓ cups (180 g) freshly grated Parmesan cheese
½ teaspoon dried oregano
1 tablespoon each finely chopped parsley and marjoram
¼ cup (60 ml) extra-virgin olive oil

Suggested wine: a dry red
(Grignolino d'Asti)

SERVES 4

PREPARATION 15 min

COOKING 20–25 min

DIFFICULTY level 1

Bell Peppers
with garlic and capers

Slice the bell peppers lengthwise into ½-inch (1-cm) strips.

Sauté the garlic with the oil in a large frying pan over medium heat. Add the bell peppers and press them down with the lid. Season with salt. Simmer over medium–low heat until the strips start to wilt, about 15 minutes. Stir from time to time with a wooden fork.

When the bell peppers are tender, turn the heat up to high add the vinegar and capers. Mix well, and until the vinegar has evaporated, 2–3 minutes.

Serve hot or at room temperature

Variation
Add 4 crumbled anchovy fillets with the vinegar and capers.
In this case, use less salt.

2 red bell peppers (capsicums), cored and seeded
1 yellow bell pepper (capsicum), cored and seeded
1 green bell pepper (capsicum), cored and seeded
3 cloves garlic, finely chopped
¼ cup (60 ml) extra-virgin olive oil
Salt
⅓ cup (90 ml) red wine vinegar
2 tablespoons salt-cured capers

Suggested wine: a young dry red (Chianti Novello)

SERVES 4–6

PREPARATION 10 min

COOKING 25 min

DIFFICULTY level 1

Baked Beans

Heat the oil in a large frying pan over medium heat. Sauté the garlic until golden, 3–4 minutes.

Add the tomatoes, sage, salt, and pepper. Simmer over medium-low heat for 15 minutes. Add the beans and simmer until heated through, 5–10 minutes.

Serve hot directly from the pot.

4 cloves garlic, finely chopped

⅓ cup (90 ml) extra-virgin olive oil

14 oz (400 g) tomatoes, peeled and chopped

8 leaves fresh sage

Salt and freshly ground black pepper

1 (14-oz/400-g) can cannellini or white kidney beans, drained

Suggested wine: a dry red (Chianti Classico)

Spring Vegetables
sicilian style

To clean the artichokes, remove all the tough outer leaves and trim the tops and stalks. Cut them in half and remove the fuzzy inner choke. Cut the tender hearts in thin wedges and soak in a bowl of cold water with the lemon juice for 10 minutes.

Heat the oil in a frying pan over medium heat and sauté the onion until softened, 3–4 minutes.

Drain the artichokes and add to the pan. Cook for 5 minutes, then add the beans, peas, and nutmeg. Season with salt and pepper and simmer over medium-low heat until tender, about 25 minutes.

Stir in the mint, sugar, and vinegar a few minutes before the beans and peas are done. Serve hot or at room temperature.

4 artichokes
Freshly squeezed juice of 1 lemon
1/4 cup (60 ml) extra-virgin olive oil
1 small onion, finely chopped
1 lb (500 g) freshly shelled fava (broad) beans
1 lb (500 g) freshly shelled peas
Pinch of nutmeg
Salt and freshly ground black pepper
1 tablespoon finely chopped mint
1 teaspoon sugar
1 teaspoon white wine vinegar

Suggested wine: a dry white (Ciclopi Bianco)

Green Beans
piedmontese style

Plunge the tomatoes into a pot of boiling water for 1 minute. Drain and place in cold water. Slip off the skins and cut in half. Squeeze out as many seeds as possible and chop coarsely.

Melt the lard in a large frying pan over medium heat. Add the garlic, basil, and parsley. Sauté over medium-high heat for 5 minutes.

Add the green beans, tomatoes, and wine, and season with salt and pepper. Cover and simmer over medium-low heat until the beans are tender, 20–30 minutes.

Serve hot or at room temperature.

1 lb (500 g) ripe tomatoes
2 tablespoons lard (or butter)
1 clove garlic, finely chopped
8 leaves fresh basil, finely chopped
2 tablespoons finely chopped parsley
2 lb (1 kg) green beans, trimmed
½ cup (125 ml) dry red wine
Salt and freshly ground black pepper

Suggested wine: a young, dry red (Barbera d'Asti)

SERVES 4

PREPARATION 25 min

COOKING 1 h 5 min

DIFFICULTY level 2

Stuffed Tomatoes

Preheat the oven to 375°F (190°C/gas 5). Cut the tops off the tomatoes using a sharp knife. Use a teaspoon to scoop out and discard the seeds. Season the tomatoes with a little salt and pepper.

Heat half the oil and half the butter in a large frying pan over low heat. Add the onion and sauté until softened, 3–4 minutes. Add the beef and sauté until lightly browned, about 5 minutes. Add the stock and simmer until the meat is almost cooked, about 10 minutes. Remove from heat.

Put the parsley, basil, garlic, and mortadella into a food processor and chop finely. Transfer to a bowl and add the meat, Parmesan, eggs, and half the bread crumbs. Season with salt and pepper and mix well.

Spoon into the hollowed out tomatoes and arrange them in an oiled baking pan. Sprinkle with the remaining bread crumbs. Dot with the remaining butter and drizzle with the remaining oil.

Bake until cooked through and lightly browned, 45 minutes. Serve hot or at room temperature.

6 large firm tomatoes
Salt and freshly ground black pepper
1/4 cup (60 ml) extra virgin olive oil
1/4 cup (60 g) butter
1 small onion, finely chopped
8 oz (250 g) lean ground (minced) beef
1/3 cup (90 ml) beef stock
    (homemade or bouillon cube)
4 tablespoons finely chopped parsley
3 tablespoons finely chopped basil
1 clove garlic
4 oz (125 g) mortadella or cooked ham
1/2 cup (60 g) freshly grated Parmesan
    cheese
2 large eggs, lightly beaten
1/2 cup (60 g) fine dry bread crumbs

Suggested wine: a dry white (Orvieto)

Braised Eggplant
with tomato and garlic

Trim the ends off the eggplants and cut them in quarters lengthwise. Slice the quarters into pieces about 1 inch (2.5 cm) long.

Sauté the garlic in the oil in a large frying pan until it turns gold, 3–4 minutes. Add the eggplant, season with salt and pepper, stir well and cover. Simmer over low heat for 10 minutes.

Add the tomatoes, mix well, and simmer for 15 minutes. Remove the lid from the pan, add the herbs, and simmer for 5 more minutes.

Serve hot. (This also makes an excellent pasta sauce).

6 eggplants (aubergines)
4 cloves garlic, finely chopped
3 tablespoons extra-virgin olive oil
Salt and freshly ground black pepper
4 medium tomatoes, peeled and chopped
2 tablespoons finely chopped parsley

Suggested wine: a dry red (Valpolicella)

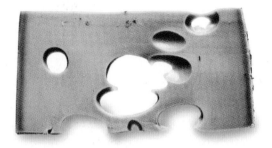

SERVES 6–8

PREPARATION 25 min

COOKING 1 h

DIFFICULTY level 2

Stuffed Vegetables

Cut the ends off the zucchini and cut them in half lengthwise. Scoop out a little of the flesh and place it in a bowl. Cut the tops off the tomatoes and scoop out the flesh with a teaspoon. Place in the bowl with the zucchini flesh.

Preheat the oven to 350°F (180°C/gas 4). Heat 2 tablespoons of oil in a large frying pan over medium heat. Add the zucchini and tomato flesh and sauté for 2–3 minutes. Add the chopped tomatoes and basil and simmer for 5 minutes. Remove from the heat and place in a bowl.

Add the cheese, eggs, salt, pepper, and enough bread crumbs to make a firm mixture.

Heat half the remaining oil in a large frying pan over medium heat. Add the hollowed out zucchini and sauté until lightly browned, 5 minutes.

Place in an oiled baking dish together with the tomatoes. Spoon the stuffing into the zucchini and tomatoes. Drizzle with the remaining oil. Bake until tender and lightly browned, 35–40 minutes. Garnish with the basil and serve hot.

4 medium zucchini (courgettes)

6 medium tomatoes, whole + 2 medium tomatoes, peeled, chopped, and pressed through a fine mesh strainer

1/3 cup (90 ml) extra-virgin olive oil

2 tablespoons finely chopped basil

8 oz (250 g) firm mild cheese, such as Fontina or Edam, coarsely grated

3 large eggs, lightly beaten

Salt and freshly ground black pepper

1/2 cup (30 g) fresh bread crumbs + a little extra, as required

Basil leaves, torn, to garnish

Suggested wine: a dry white (Vernaccia di San Gimignano)

Pea Mousse

Bring 2 quarts (2 liters) of salted water to a boil in a pan and cook the peas and onion for 10 minutes. Drain well and set aside to cool.

Place the caprino, peas, onion and oil in a food processor and chop until the mixture is creamy. Season with salt and pepper.

Line a 4 cup (1-liter) pudding mold with plastic wrap (cling film) and pour the mixture in, pressing with a spoon to eliminate pockets of air. Knock the mold against a work surface to eliminate air bubbles.

Chill in the refrigerator for at least 2 hours. Invert onto a round serving dish and, if liked, garnish with the cherry tomatoes and parsley.

- 1 lb (500 g) fresh or frozen peas
- 1 medium onion, cut in half
- 1 lb (500 g) fresh, creamy caprino (goat) cheese
- 3 tablespoons extra-virgin olive oil
- Salt and freshly ground black pepper
- 8 cherry tomatoes, cut in quarters (optional)
- 8 tiny sprigs parsley (optional)

Suggested wine: a dry red (Cabernet Sauvignon)

Spinach Soufflé

Preheat the oven to 350°F (180°C/gas 4). Butter an 8-inch (20 cm) soufflé mold and sprinkle with the bread crumbs.

Rinse the spinach under cold running water. Do not drain. Cook over medium heat with just the water left clinging to the leaves, for 5 minutes. Chop finely in a food processor.

Place the spinach in a small frying pan over medium heat with $1/4$ cup (60 g) of butter and simmer until all the butter has been absorbed.

Combine the spinach with the Parmesan and egg yolks in a bowl. Mix until smooth.

Beat the egg whites with a pinch of salt until very stiff. Fold them into the spinach mixture. Place half the spinach mixture in the mold and cover with the anchovy fillets. Cover with the remaining spinach. Chop the remaining butter and scatter over the top of the soufflé.

Bake for 30 minutes. Serve immediately.

$1/3$ cup (90 g) butter

3 tablespoons fine dry bread crumbs

$1\frac{1}{2}$ lb (750 g) fresh spinach leaves, tough stalks removed

4 tablespoons freshly grated Parmesan cheese

3 eggs, separated

Salt

8 salt-cured anchovy fillets

Suggested wine: a dry red (Torgiano Rosso)

Capri Salad

Cut the tomatoes in thick slices and arrange on a flat serving dish.

Cut the mozzarella in slices of the same width and alternate with the tomato. Sprinkle with basil, salt, and pepper, and drizzle with the oil.

Serve at once.

8 large ripe salad tomatoes
1 lb (500 g) fresh mozzarella cheese
20 large basil leaves, torn
Salt and freshly ground black pepper
1/3 cup (90 ml) extra-virgin olive oil

Suggested wine: a light dry white
   (Capri Bianco)

Mixed Salad

SERVES 4

PREPARATION 10 min

DIFFICULTY level 1

Place the tomatoes, bell peppers, cucumber, radishes, red onion, fava beans, olives, garlic, and celery in a large salad bowl. Toss well.

Beat together the basil, oil, vinegar, and salt in a small bowl.

Add the tuna to the salad. Drizzle with the dressing and toss well. Discard the garlic.

Arrange the eggs, artichokes, and anchovy fillets on top of the salad in a decorative manner. Serve at room temperature.

3 ripe tomatoes, cut into segments

2 bell peppers (capsicums), seeded and sliced

1 cucumber, peeled and sliced

10 radishes, cut into quarters

1 small red onion, sliced

8 oz (250 g) fresh fava (broad) beans, shelled

20 black olives, pitted

10 green olives, pitted

2 cloves garlic, lightly crushed but whole

1 stalk celery, finely chopped

6 basil leaves, torn

1/4 cup (60 ml) extra-virgin olive oil

3 tablespoons white wine vinegar

Salt

8 oz (250 g) canned tuna, broken into pieces

3 hard-boiled eggs, shelled and cut into segments

5 artichoke hearts preserved in oil, drained and cut into segments

10 salt-cured anchovy fillets, rinsed

Suggested wine: a dry white (Cinque Terre)

DESSERTS

Tiramisù

This is the traditional Italian recipe which makes use of raw eggs. If you wish to avoid the health risks associated with raw eggs, be sure to use pasteurized eggs.

Whisk the egg yolks and sugar until pale and creamy. Carefully fold in the mascarpone.

Beat the egg whites with the salt until very stiff and fold them into the mixture. Spread a thin layer over the bottom of a large oval serving dish.

Soak the ladyfingers briefly in the coffee and place a layer over the cream on the bottom of the dish. Cover with another layer of the cream and sprinkle with a little chocolate.

Continue in this way until all the ingredients are in the dish. Finish with a layer of cream and chocolate and dust with the cocoa powder.

Chill in the refrigerator for at least 3 hours before serving.

5 eggs, separated
1 cup (200 g) granulated sugar
2 cups (500 g) mascarpone cheese
$1/4$ teaspoon salt
About 30 ladyfingers
1 cup (250 ml) strong cold black coffee
7 oz (200 g) semi-sweet (dark) chocolate, grated
2 tablespoons unsweetened cocoa powder

Suggested wine: a dry sparkling rosé (Sudtiroler Spumante Rosato)

Florentine Trifle

Mix the sugar and water in a saucepan over medium heat until the sugar has dissolved and it comes to a boil. Boil for 5 minutes. Remove from the heat. Add the brandy and rum and let cool.

Moisten the sides of a domed 1½-quart (1.5-liter) pudding mold with a little of the sugar syrup and line with half the cake slices. Brush with the syrup.

Beat the cream until stiff. Gently fold the confectioners' sugar, nuts, candied fruit, and grated chocolate into the cream. Spoon the cream into the mold and top with the cake slices.

Cover the top of the mold with aluminum foil to seal. Place in the freezer for at least 4 hours.

Dip the mold into cold water. Invert onto a serving plate.

1 cup (200 g) granulated sugar
1 cup (250 ml) water
3 tablespoons brandy
3 tablespoons rum
1 Italian sponge cake (see page 316), cut into ¼-inch (5-mm) thick slices
2 cups (500 ml) heavy (double) cream
⅓ cup (50 g) confectioners' (icing) sugar
⅓ cup (50 g) finely ground almonds
⅓ cup (50 g) finely ground hazelnuts
¼ cup (50 g) mixed candied fruit, chopped
6 oz (180 g) semisweet (dark) chocolate, grated

Suggested wine: a sweet white (Trentino Moscato Giallo)

SERVES 4–6

PREPARATION 10 min + 1 h to rest

COOKING 30 min

DIFFICULTY level 1

Crêpes
with redcurrants and rum

Crêpes: Place the flour and salt in a medium bowl. Beat in the eggs one at a time. Gradually add the milk, beating until smooth. Set the batter aside to rest for 1 hour.

Melt 1 teaspoon of butter in a crêpe pan and add 2–3 tablespoons of batter. Swivel the pan so that the batter coats the base of the pan evenly.

Cook until lightly browned, about 2 minutes. Turn the crêpe using a palette knife and cook the other side until lightly browned. Slip onto a plate. Repeat until all the batter is cooked. Stack the cooked crêpes and place in a war oven.

Filling: Melt the preserves in a small saucepan over low heat. Stir in the rum. Remove from the heat. Beat the cream in a large bowl until stiff.

Spread each crêpe with a layer of preserves. Fold in half and then in half again to form triangles. Arrange on serving dishes. Decorate with whipped cream and the fresh red currants. Serve at once.

Crêpes
1/2 cup (75 g) all-purpose (plain) flour
1/4 teaspoon salt
4 large eggs
1 cup (250 ml) milk
3 tablespoons butter

Filling
1 1/2 cups (375 g) redcurrant (or other berry fruit) preserves (jam)
1 tablespoon rum
1/2 cup (125 ml) heavy (double) cream
Fresh redcurrants, to garnish

Suggested wine: a sweet white (Colli Euganei Moscato)

Crêpes
with raspberries and pastry cream

Prepare the crêpes. Place the raspberries in a bowl with the Cointreau, 1 tablespoon of confectioners' sugar, and the orange zest. Set aside.

Pastry Cream: Bring the milk to a boil in a large saucepan over low heat. Beat the flour, sugar, and egg yolks in a medium bowl. Stir in the Cointreau. Add the boiling milk, beating constantly. Return to the saucepan. Simmer over low heat, stirring constantly, until thickened, about 5 minutes. Stir in the hazelnuts and remove from the heat.

Spread each crêpe with some pastry cream and cover with raspberries. Roll up the crêpes and dust with the remaining confectioners' sugar. Garnish with raspberries and hazelnuts and serve hot.

1 quantity crêpes (see page 278)
12 oz (350 g) fresh raspberries
+ extra, to garnish
3 tablespoons Cointreau
1/4 cup (30 g) confectioners' (icing) sugar
Grated zest of 1 orange

Pastry Cream
1 1/4 cups (300 ml) milk
2 tablespoons all-purpose (plain) flour
1/4 cup (50 g) granulated sugar
2 large egg yolks
2 tablespoons Cointreau
1/2 cup (50 g) finely chopped toasted hazelnuts, + extra, to garnish

Suggested wine: a sweet white
(Vin Santo di Montepulciano)

Hazelnut Cake
with fresh fruit

Set out a 9-inch (23-cm) springform pan. Bring the milk to a boil in a saucepan over low heat. Remove from the heat.

Beat the egg yolks, sugar, and vanilla in a large bowl with an electric mixer at high speed until pale and thick. With mixer at low speed, gradually add the cornstarch.

Pour the hot milk into the egg mixture. Return the mixture to the saucepan over low heat and cook, stirring constantly with a wooden spoon, until thickened, 5–10 minutes. Let cool a little then stir the hazelnut cream into the custard.

Line the springform pan with half the ladyfingers and cover with custard. Repeat. Refrigerate for 8 hours.

Loosen and remove the pan sides. Decorate the top of the cake with the fruit and serve.

1 quart (1 liter) milk

6 large egg yolks

1 cup (200 g) granulated sugar

1 teaspoon vanilla extract (essence)

$^1/_3$ cup (50 g) + 2 tablespoons cornstarch (cornflour)

28 ladyfingers

$^1/_3$ cup (90 g) chocolate hazelnut cream (Nutella)

$^1/_2$ cup (125 g) sliced fresh fruit (such as strawberries, kiwifruit, bananas, or pineapple), to decorate

Suggested wine: a sweet, lightly sparkling white (Oltrepo Pavese Moscato)

Crème Caramel

Preheat the oven to 350°F (180°C/gas 4). Beat the eggs and egg yolks with 1¼ cups (150 g) of sugar until very pale and creamy.

Heat the milk and vanilla to boiling point over medium heat. Remove from heat and pour into the eggs and sugar. Stir well until the sugar dissolves.

Place the remaining sugar in a small saucepan with the water over very low heat until it turns to caramel, about 10 minutes.

Pour the caramel into 1-quart (1-liter) pudding mold. Strain the milk and egg mixture into the same mold.

Place the mold in a roasting pan half-filled with water. Bake in the water bath until set, 50–60 minutes.

Leave to cool, then chill for at least 3 hours in the refrigerator before unmolding to serve.

2 large eggs + 3 large egg yolks
1 cup (200 g) granulated sugar
2⅓ cups (650 ml) milk
½ teaspoon vanilla extract (essence)
2 tablespoons cold water

Suggested wine: a dry or medium white
    (Pagadebit di Romagna)

Frozen Trifle

Set out a domed 1½-quart (1.5-liter) pudding mold.

Warm the milk and lemon zest in a saucepan over medium heat. Beat the egg yolks and ¾ cup (150 g) of sugar in a large bowl with an electric mixer at high speed until pale and thick.

Discard the lemon zest from the warmed milk. Stir warm milk and flour into the egg mixture. Return the mixture to the saucepan and bring to a boil, stirring constantly, over medium heat. Simmer, stirring constantly, until thick, 5–10 minutes. Add the vanilla. Transfer half of the mixture to a medium bowl.

Melt the chocolate in a double boiler over barely simmering water. Stir the chocolate into one of the bowls.

Cook the remaining sugar and water in a saucepan over medium heat until the sugar has dissolved. Remove from the heat and add the liqueur.

Line the pudding mold with half the cake slices. Drizzle with the sugar and liqueur syrup. Spoon the vanilla filling into the mold. Top with half the remaining cake slices. Spoon the chocolate mixture over the top. Cover with the remaining cake slices.

Place in the freezer for at least 4 hours.

Dip the mold briefly into cold water. Invert onto a serving plate.

2 cups (500 ml) milk
Zest of ½ lemon, in one long piece
4 large egg yolks
1 cup (200 g) granulated sugar
1 tablespoon all-purpose (plain) flour
1 teaspoon vanilla extract (essence)
5 oz (150 g) semisweet (dark) chocolate, coarsely chopped
¼ cup (60 ml) water
⅔ cup (180 ml) Alchermes liqueur or Marsala wine
1 Italian sponge cake (see page 316), cut into ¼-inch (5-mm) thick slices

Suggested wine: a sweet white (Moscato di Noto)

SERVES 6

PREPARATION 20 min + 3 h 30 min to chill

COOKING 5 min

DIFFICULTY level 1

Lemon Sorbet
with fresh fruit

Place the sugar and water in a saucepan and bring to a boil. Simmer for 3–4 minutes, then set aside to cool. Stir in the juice of 4 lemons when the mixture is completely cool.

Whisk the egg whites and salt until very stiff in a freezerproof bowl. Gradually stir in the lemon syrup. If you have an ice-cream maker, pour into the machine and freeze according to the manufacturers' instructions.

If you do not have an ice-cream maker, place the bowl in the freezer. Stir every 30 minutes to make sure it freezes evenly. After three hours whisk the mixture, then return to the freezer for another 30 minutes.

Serve in individual dishes with the thinly sliced fruit sprinkled with sugar and the remaining lemon juice. If liked, vary the fresh fruit according to what is in season.

1 cup (200 g) granulated sugar
2¼ cups (300 ml) water
Freshly squeezed juice of 5 lemons
3 large egg whites
⅛ teaspoon salt
3 large peaches, thinly sliced
4 apricots, thinly sliced
2 tablespoons granulated sugar

Suggested wine: a sweet white
(Malvasia delle Lipari)

SERVES 4

PREPARATION 10 min

COOKING 25 min

DIFFICULTY level 1

Zabaglione
with cream and raspberries

Beat the egg yolks and brown sugar in a double boiler until creamy. Add ¼ cup (60 ml) of Marsala and beat with a whisk until smooth.

Place the double boiler over barely simmering water and beat with the whisk until thickened, about 15 minutes. Remove from the heat and let cool.

Beat the mascarpone in a medium bowl with half the cream. Add the remaining Marsala and whisk until light and creamy. Fold the zabaglione carefully into this mixture.

Divide almost all the raspberries among four dessert bowls. Top with zabaglione and the remaining cream. Decorate with the remaining raspberries and serve.

3 large egg yolks
¾ cup (150 g) firmly packed dark brown
    sugar
¾ cup (180 ml) dry Marsala wine
½ cup (125 g) mascarpone cheese
½ cup (125 ml) heavy (double) cream
12 oz (350 g) fresh raspberries

Suggested wine: a sweet white
    (Malvasia di Casorzo d'Asti)

Strawberry Pie

Sweet Shortcrust Pastry: Place the flour and salt in a large bowl. Add the sugar and lemon zest. Rub in the butter using your fingertips until the mixture resembles bread crumbs. Add the egg and port and mix to make a smooth dough. Wrap in plastic wrap (cling film) and chill in the refrigerator for 30 minutes.

Preheat the oven to 400°F (200°C/gas 6). Butter a 10-inch (25-cm) pie pan.

Roll out the pastry on a floured work surface and use it to line the prepared pan. Cover with waxed paper and fill with dried beans or pie weights. Bake blind for 30 minutes. Let cool. Discard the beans and waxed paper.

Pastry Cream: Bring the milk to a boil in a large saucepan. Beat the egg yolks, flour, and sugar in a large bowl until pale and creamy. Add the hot milk and beat well. Return the mixture to the pan and simmer, stirring constantly, until thickened, 5–7 minutes. Add the vanilla.

Remove from the heat and let cool slightly. Pour into the pastry case. Let cool a little then chill in the refrigerator for 1 hour.

Top with the strawberries and brush with the apricot preserves.

Sweet Shortcrust Pastry
1⅓ cups (200 g) all-purpose (plain) flour
⅛ teaspoon salt
½ cup (100 g) granulated sugar
Finely grated zest of 1 lemon
⅓ cup (90 g) cold butter, cut up
1 large egg, lightly beaten
2 tablespoons port

Pastry Cream
1¼ cups (300 ml) milk
2 large egg yolks
2 tablespoons all-purpose (plain) flour
½ cup (100 g) granulated sugar
1 teaspoon vanilla extract (essence)

12 oz (350 g) strawberries, sliced
½ cup (125 g) apricot preserves (jam), melted

Suggested wine: a sweet white
   (Colli Euganei Moscato)

SERVES 6

PREPARATION 10 min

COOKING 25 min

DIFFICULTY level 2

Baked Zabaglione
cake with orange

Preheat the oven to 425°F (220°C/gas 7). Brush an 8–10 inch (20–25 cm) round ovenproof dish with 1 tablespoon of the liqueur. Cut the sponge cake to the same size as the dish and then fit it into the dish.

Mix the orange juice and remaining liqueur in a small bowl. Drizzle one-third of this mixture over the sponge cake.

Beat the egg yolks and sugar in a large bowl until pale and creamy. Transfer to a double boiler over barely simmering water. Gradually add the liqueur mixture, beating constantly, until thickened, 10–15 minutes.

Pour the zabaglione over the sponge cake. Dust with the confectioners' sugar and sprinkle with almonds.

Bake until the top is golden brown, 5–10 minutes. Remove from the oven. Decorate with orange zest and mint. Serve hot.

¼ cup (60 ml) orange liqueur
1 Italian sponge cake (see page 316)
Freshly squeezed juice of 3 oranges, filtered
4 large egg yolks
½ cup (100 g) granulated sugar
¼ cup (30 g) confectioners' (icing) sugar
¼ cup (25 g) flaked almonds
1 orange, thinly sliced, to decorate
Sprig of mint, to decorate

Suggested wine: a sweet white
    (Golfo del Tigullio Moscato)

Panna Cotta
with caramel sauce

Oil 6 ramekins. Place the cream, ½ cup (100 g) of sugar, and vanilla pod in a large saucepan. Bring to a boil over low heat. Remove from the heat and add the gelatin. Stir until completely dissolved. Discard the vanilla.

Divide the cream mixture among the prepared ramekins, let cool, then chill in the refrigerator for at least 4 hours.

Place the remaining sugar and water in a separate saucepan and cook over low heat until the sugar has caramelized, 5–10 minutes.

Let the ramekins stand in a basin of boiling water for 1 minute before turning the panna cotta out onto serving dishes. Drizzle with the caramel sauce and serve.

3 cups (750 ml) heavy (double) cream
1 cup (200 g) granulated sugar
1 vanilla pod
1 tablespoon gelatin powder
2 tablespoons water

Suggested wine: a sweet white
(Moscato di Trani)

SERVES 6

PREPARATION 15 min + 4 h to chill

COOKING 10 min

DIFFICULTY level 2

Panna Cotta
with raspberry sauce

Oil 6 ramekins. Place the milk, cream, and $\frac{1}{2}$ cup (100 g) of sugar in a large saucepan. Bring to a boil over low heat. Remove from the heat and add the gelatin and almond liqueur. Stir until the gelatin is dissolved.

Divide the mixture among the prepared ramekins and chill in the refrigerator for at least 4 hours.

Place the remaining sugar and water in a separate saucepan and simmer over medium-low heat until the sugar has dissolved. Add the cinnamon, raspberries, and wine and simmer for 5 minutes. Remove from the heat, discard the cinnamon stick, and strain to remove the raspberry pips. Let cool then chill in the refrigerator

Let the ramekins stand in a basin of boiling water for 1 minute before turning the panna cotta out onto serving dishes. Spoon the raspberry sauce over the top and serve.

$1\frac{1}{2}$ cups (375 ml) milk
$1\frac{1}{2}$ cups (375 ml) heavy (double) cream
$1\frac{1}{2}$ cups (300 g) granulated sugar
1 tablespoon gelatin powder
2 tablespoons almond liqueur
1 cup (250 ml) water
1 cinnamon stick
12 oz (350 g) fresh raspberries
$\frac{1}{2}$ cup (125 ml) high-quality dry red wine

Suggested wine: a sweet white
   (Moscato di Cagliari)

CAKES & COOKIES

Chocolate Cake
with cherry cream filling

Preheat the oven to 350°F (180°C/gas 4). Butter two 9-inch (23-cm) round pans.

Place the flour and baking powder in a large bowl. Melt the chocolate and water in a double boiler over barely simmering water.

Beat the butter and brown sugar in a large bowl until creamy. Add the eggs, one at a time, beating until just blended after each addition. Gradually beat in the chocolate mixture, sour cream, and dry ingredients.

Spoon the batter into the prepared pans. Bake until a toothpick inserted into the center comes out clean, 35–45 minutes.

Let cool in the pans on racks for 10 minutes. Turn out onto the racks and let cool completely. Split the cakes horizontally.

Cherry Cream Filling: Mix the preserves and kirsch. Beat the cream in a large bowl until stiff.

Chocolate Frosting: Stir together the confectioners' sugar and cocoa in a double boiler. Add the butter, vanilla, and enough of the water to make a firm paste. Stir over simmering water until smooth, about 3 minutes.

To Assemble: Place one layer of cake on a serving plate. Spread with one-third of the preserves and one-third of the whipped cream. Repeat with the remaining cake layers, finishing with a plain layer.

Spread the frosting over the top and sides of the cake. Decorate with the cherries.

$1^2/_3$ cups (250 g) all-purpose (plain) flour
$1^1/_2$ teaspoons baking powder
5 oz (150 g) semisweet (dark) chocolate, chopped
$^1/_2$ cup (125 ml) water
$^1/_2$ cup (125 g) butter
$1^1/_4$ cups (250 g) firmly packed dark brown sugar
2 large eggs
$^1/_2$ cup (125 ml) sour cream

Cherry Cream Filling
1 cup (250 g) cherry preserves (jam)
3 tablespoons kirsch
2 cups (500 ml) heavy (double) cream

Chocolate Frosting
2 cups (300 g) confectioners' (icing) sugar
4 tablespoons unsweetened cocoa powder
2 tablespoons butter, softened
1 teaspoon vanilla extract (essence)
2–3 tablespoons boiling water

Candied cherries, to decorate

Suggested wine: a sweet white (Moscato di Cagliari)

Panforte

Preheat the oven to 350°F (180°C/gas 4). Line a baking sheet with rice paper. Mix the candied peels, nuts, flour, and spices in a large bowl.

Heat the brown sugar, honey, and water in a medium saucepan over medium heat, stirring constantly, until the sugar has dissolved. Wash down the sides of the pan with a pastry brush dipped in cold water to prevent sugar crystals from forming. Simmer, without stirring, until small bubbles form on the surface and the syrup registers 234°F (114°C) on a candy thermometer. Remove from the heat and beat into the nut mixture.

Spoon onto the prepared sheet. Shape the dough into a round about $^{1}/_{2}$-inch (1-cm) thick.

Bake until golden brown, about 35 minutes.

Cool the cake completely on the baking sheet. Remove the excess rice paper from the edges before serving. Dust with the confectioners' sugar, if liked.

1 cup (100 g) candied orange peel, coarsely chopped

2 tablespoons candied lemon peel, chopped

8 oz (250 g) unblanched, toasted almonds, coarsely chopped

1 cup (100 g) walnuts, coarsely chopped

1 cup (150 g) all-purpose (plain) flour

1 teaspoon each ground coriander, mace, and nutmeg

$^{1}/_{4}$ teaspoons cloves

1 cup (200 g) firmly packed brown sugar

$^{1}/_{2}$ cup (125 ml) honey

$^{1}/_{2}$ cup (125 ml) water

4 tablespoons confectioners' (icing) sugar, to dust (optional)

Suggested wine: a sweet white (Moscato di Cagliari)

SERVES 10–12

PREPARATION 20 min + 3 h to rise

COOKING 30 min

DIFFICULTY level 2

Florentine Sponge

Dissolve the yeast in a little of the warm water.

Place the flour in a large bowl and pour in the yeast mixture. Mix until the flour has all been absorbed, adding enough of the remaining water to obtain a smooth dough.

Transfer to a lightly floured work surface and knead for 5 minutes.

Wrap in a clean kitchen towel and leave in a warm place to rise for 1 hour.

Knead the dough again, adding the eggs, sugar, butter, orange zest, and salt as you work.

Butter and flour a jelly-roll (swiss roll) pan. Spoon the dough into the pan. Leave to rise for 2 hours.

Preheat the oven to 350°F (180°C/gas 4). Bake until golden brown, about 30 minutes. Let cool in the pan. Dust with confectioners' sugar.

I oz (30 g) fresh yeast or 2 ($\frac{1}{4}$-oz/7-g) packages active dry yeast
I cup (250 ml) lukewarm water
4 cups (600 g) all-purpose plain flour, sifted
4 large eggs
$\frac{3}{4}$ cup (150 g) granulated sugar
$\frac{1}{2}$ cup (125 g) butter, melted
Finely grated zest of I orange
$\frac{1}{4}$ teaspoon salt
4 tablespoons confectioners' (icing) sugar

Suggested wine: a sweet white (Moscadello di Montalcino)

Polenta Cake
with lemon

SERVES 6–8
PREPARATION 20 min
COOKING 40 min
DIFFICULTY level 1

Preheat the oven to 375°F (190°C/gas 5). Butter and flour a 12 x 3-inch (30 x 8.5 cm) fluted tube pan. Melt the butter over very low heat and set aside to cool.

Beat the butter and sugar in an electric mixer on medium speed until pale and creamy. Beat in the eggs and egg yolks one at a time

With mixer on low, add the lemon liqueur, almonds, polenta, flour, lemon zest, baking powder, and vanilla. Spoon the batter into the prepared pan.

Bake until golden brown, about 40 minutes. Let cool in the pan for 5 minutes then turn out onto a cake rack and let cool completely. Dust with confectioners' sugar just before serving.

1 cup (250 g) butter
2½ cups (375 g) confectioners' (icing) sugar, + extra, to dust
3 large eggs + 6 large egg yolks
2 tablespoons Limoncello (lemon liqueur)
1 cup (100 g) finely ground almonds
1½ cups (275 g) polenta (stoneground cornmeal)
1 cup (150 g) all-purpose (plain) flour
Freshly grated zest of 1 lemon
1 teaspoon baking powder
¼ teaspoon vanilla extract (essence)

Suggested wine: a sweet, lightly sparkling white (Brachetto d'Acqui)

Apricot Tart

Preheat the oven to 375°F (190°C/gas 5).

Roll the pastry out on a lightly floured work surface in a 12-inch (30-cm) round. Line the base and sides of a 10-inch (25-cm) tart pan, trimming the edges if needed. Line with a sheet of waxed paper and fill with dried beans or pie weights.

Bake blind for 20 minutes. Discard the paper and beans or pie weights. Let cool completely. Refrigerate for 1 hour.

Arrange the cake slices in the pastry shell. Drizzle with 1 tablespoon of wine. Arrange the apricot slices on top.

Beat the egg yolks, sugar, and remaining wine with an electric mixer at medium speed until pale and thick. Spoon the egg mixture over the apricots. Dust with the confectioners' sugar.

Bake until lightly browned, about 15 minutes. Cool the tart in the pan for 15 minutes. Dust with confectioners' sugar and serve warm.

1 quantity sweet shortcrust pastry (see page 289)

1 Italian sponge cake (see page 316), thinly sliced

2 tablespoons sweet dessert wine

1 lb (500 g) apricots, peeled, pitted, and thinly sliced

4 large egg yolks

$\frac{1}{4}$ cup (50 g) granulated sugar

2 tablespoons confectioners' (icing) sugar, to dust

Suggested wine: a sweet white (Moscato di Pantelleria)

Fruit Crostata

Place the flour, sugar, and salt in a large bowl. Cut in the butter with your fingertips until the mixture resembles coarse crumbs. Add the egg yolk and water and mix to form a smooth dough.

Shape into a ball, wrap in plastic wrap (cling film), and refrigerate for 30 minutes. Preheat the oven to 375°F (190°C/gas 5).

Roll the dough out on a lightly floured surface to a 12-inch (30-cm) disk. Line the base and sides of a 9-inch (23-cm) tart pan, trimming the edges if needed. Line the pastry shell with a sheet of waxed paper and fill with dried beans or pie weights.

Bake for 15 minutes. Discard the paper and beans or pie weights. Bake until golden brown, about 15 minutes. Let cool completely.

Topping: Spoon the pastry cream into the pastry case. Arrange the fruit on top and brush with the preserves. Serve as soon as possible so that the pastry does not become soggy.

Pastry
1 cup (150 g) all-purpose (plain) flour
2 tablespoons granulated sugar
1/8 teaspoon salt
1/3 cup (90 g) cold butter, cut up
1 large egg yolk
1 tablespoon iced water

Topping
1 quantity pastry cream (see page 289)
2 cups (500 g) sliced fresh fruit or whole berries
1/4 cup (80 g) apricot preserves (jam), warmed

Suggested wine: a sweet white (Moscato d'Asti)

Prato Cookies

Preheat the oven to 400°F (200°C/gas 6). Butter and flour 2 cookie sheets. Spread the almonds on a baking sheet and bake for 3–4 minutes. When cool enough to handle, skin and chop coarsely. Lower the oven temperature to 375°F (190°C/gas 5).

Beat the egg yolks and sugar together in a mixing bowl until pale and creamy. Stir in the flour, almonds, salt, and almond extract gradually, using a fork and then combining by hand. Beat the egg whites in a large bowl until stiff and fold into the mixture. Knead the mixture quickly but thoroughly on a floured work surface.

Shape the dough into long cylinders about ½-inch (1-cm) in diameter. Transfer to the prepared cookie sheets. Bake for 25 minutes. Remove from the oven and raise the temperature to 400°F (200°C/gas 6). Slice the cylinders diagonally into pieces 1½-inches (4-cm) long, and return to until pale golden brown, about 10 minutes. Let cool before serving.

8 oz (250 g) almonds, unpeeled

4 large eggs, separated

2½ cups (500 g) granulated sugar

3⅓ cups (500 g) all-purpose (plain) flour

¼ teaspoon salt

½ teaspoon almond extract (essence)

Suggested wine: a sweet, medium or dry
dessert wine (Vin Santo)

Siena Cookies

Preheat the oven to 400°F (200°C/gas 6). Line two baking sheets with rice paper.

Spread the almonds on a baking sheet and bake for 3–4 minutes. Transfer to a food processor and chop finely. Place in a large bowl and stir in both sugars, the orange zest, and almond extract. Mix well, then carefully fold in the egg white.

Place spoonfuls of the mixture on the prepared baking sheets and refrigerate for 10 hours.

Preheat the oven to 300°F (150°C/gas 2). Bake for 1 hour, reducing the heat if they begin to brown. They should be pale and soft when cooked.

Remove from the oven and dust generously with the extra confectioners' sugar. Serve cool.

8 oz (250 g) almonds, unpeeled

1 cup (200 g) granulated sugar

1 cup (150 g) confectioners' (icing) sugar, + extra to dust

4 tablespoons finely chopped candied orange zest

$1/2$ teaspoon almond extract (essence)

1 egg white, stiffly beaten

Suggested wine: a sweet white (Bianco Pisano di San Torpè Vin Santo)

Pumpkin Fritters

Soak the raisins in the Marsala for 10 minutes, then drain.

Cut the pumpkin in half and remove the seeds and fibrous matter. Peel, then chop the flesh into large pieces.

Place in a saucepan with enough cold water to cover. Cover the pan and cook over medium heat until the pumpkin is just tender, about 15 minutes. Drain well and wrap in a cloth to absorb any excess moisture.

Place in a bowl and mash until smooth with a fork or potato masher. Add the raisins, ½ cup (100 g) of sugar, lemon zest, and salt. Add the flour and baking powder and mix thoroughly.

Scoop out spoonfuls of the mixture and shape into fritters about the size of a flattened walnut.

Heat the oil in a deep fryer. Fry the fritters in batches, removing them with a slotted spoon when golden brown all over, 5–7 minutes each batch. Drain on paper towels.

Sprinkle with sugar and serve hot.

6 oz (180 g) seedless golden raisins (sultanas)
1 cup (250 ml) sweet Marsala wine
2½ lb (1.25 kg) pumpkin or winter squash
1 cup (200 g) granulated sugar
Finely grated zest of 1 lemon
⅛ teaspoon salt
1⅓ cups (200 g) all-purpose (plain) flour
1 tablespoon baking powder
3 cups (750 ml) olive oil, for frying

Suggested wine: a sweet white (Vin Santo dei Colli Piacentini)

Sicilian Cannoli

You will need cannolo molds to prepare these traditional Sicilian filled fritters.

Filling: Press the ricotta through a fine mesh strainer. Mix the ricotta, sugar, candied peel, orange blossom water, and chocolate in a large bowl. Divide the mixture into 2 bowls. Add the cocoa to one of the bowls and mix well.

Pastry: Mix the flour, sugar, cocoa, Marsala, coffee, and salt in a large bowl to make a soft dough. Cover the dough and chill in the refrigerator for 1 hour.

Roll out the dough on a lightly floured surface to 1/8-inch (3-mm) thick. Cut into ovals large enough to wrap around the cannoli molds. Wrap an oval of pastry around each mold. Overlap the pastry where it meets and seal each one using a little of the egg white.

Heat the oil in a deep fryer over medium heat. Fry the pastry coated tubes until the pastry is golden brown, 3–4 minutes.

Drain on paper towels and let cool. Slip the pastry cases off the molds.

Fill each cannolo with the plain ricotta mixture from one end and the chocolate ricotta mixture from the other end. Garnish by pressing pieces of candied peel and cherries into the filling at the ends of each cannolo.

Dust with confectioners' sugar and serve.

Filling
14 oz (400 g) fresh ricotta cheese, drained
1 cup (200 g) granulated sugar
3/4 cup (75 g) chopped candied peel
2 tablespoons orange blossom water or orange liqueur
2 oz (60 g) semisweet (dark) chocolate, finely chopped
1 tablespoon unsweetened cocoa powder

Pastry
1 2/3 cups (250 g) all-purpose (plain) flour
1 tablespoon sugar
1 tablespoon unsweetened cocoa powder
1/3 cup (90 ml) dry Marsala wine
1 teaspoon instant coffee (optional)
1/8 teaspoon salt

1 quart (1 liter) olive oil, for frying

To Garnish
Candied peel
Glacé cherries
2 tablespoons confectioners' (icing) sugar

Suggested wine: a sweet white (Moscato di Pantelleria)

SERVES 8–10

PREPARATION 15 min

COOKING 25 min

DIFFICULTY level 2

Carnival Cookies

Place the flour and salt in a large bowl. Mix in the eggs, sugar, lemon zest, wine, and the extra-virgin oil to form a stiff dough.

Roll the dough out on a lightly floured work surface and cut into strips about 1 x 6-inches (2.5 x 15-cm).

Heat the oil in a deep fryer until very hot. Fry the cookies in small batches until crisp and golden brown, 5–7 minutes each batch.

Drain well on paper towels. Dust with the confectioners' sugar and serve.

3 cups (450 g) all-purpose (plain) flour
1/8 teaspoon salt
2 large eggs
2 tablespoons granulated sugar
Finely grated zest of 1 lemon
1 tablespoon dry white wine
1 tablespoon extra-virgin olive oil
3 cups (750 ml) olive oil, for frying
1/3 cup (50 g) confectioners' (icing) sugar

Suggested wine: a sweet red
    (Malvasia di Castelnuovo Don Bosco)

Frosted Cassata

Bring the sugar, water, and vanilla bean to a boil in a saucepan over medium heat. Cook, stirring frequently, until the sugar has completely dissolved. Set aside to cool, then discard the vanilla bean.

Beat the ricotta in a large bowl with an electric mixer at high speed until smooth. Gradually stir in the syrup. Stir in the chocolate, candied fruit, pistachios, and kirsch.

Line a 9-inch (23-cm) springform pan with slices of sponge cake. Warm 2 tablespoons apricot preserves and brush over the cake slices. Spread with a layer of the ricotta mixture. Top with another layer of sponge cake slices. Refrigerate for 2 hours.

Loosen and remove the pan sides. Invert onto a serving plate and remove the pan bottom.

Warm the remaining apricot preserves, orange-flower water, and 1 tablespoon of confectioners' sugar in a saucepan over low heat until syrupy. Drizzle the glaze over the cake.

Warm the fondant and gradually work in the green food coloring (if preferred, leave the green food coloring out and make a white icing). Roll the fondant out and spread over the cake.

Mix the remaining confectioners' sugar with the warm water in a small bowl until a slightly liquid frosting is formed (if you have used white fondant icing, color the frosting green or red). Spoon into a plastic pastry bag. Cut off the end to create a tiny opening. Pipe over the cake in swirling patterns.

Decorate with the whole pieces of candied fruit.

1¼ cups (250 g) granulated sugar

½ cup (125 ml) water

1 whole vanilla bean

1 lb (500 g) ricotta cheese, drained and pressed through a strainer

5 oz (150 g) bittersweet (dark) chocolate, finely chopped

1½ cups (150 g) mixed candied fruit, chopped + whole pieces, to decorate

2 tablespoons pistachios

2 tablespoons kirsch

1 Italian Sponge Cake (see page 316), thinly sliced

½ cup (120 g) apricot preserves (jam)

2 tablespoons orange-flower water

1 cup (150 g) confectioners' (icing) sugar

2 cups (400 g) fondant (icing)

Green food coloring

¼ cup (60 ml) lukewarm water

Suggested wine: a sweet white (Moscato di Pantelleria)

Raspberry Cream
layer cake

Italian Sponge Cake: Preheat the oven to 425°F (220°C/gas 7). Line a 10-inch (24-cm) springform pan with parchment paper.

Beat the eggs and sugar in a large bowl until pale and creamy. Gradually fold in the flour and baking powder.

Spoon the batter into the prepared pan. Bake until golden brown and springy to the touch, 7–10 minutes. Remove from the oven and cool on a rack for 5 minutes. Turn out of the pan, remove the parchment paper, and let cool completely.

Filling: Place the raspberries, 1 cup (150 g) of confectioners' sugar, and kirsch in a large bowl. Soak for 1 hour. Drain the raspberries, reserving the syrup.

Beat the mascarpone remaining confectioners' sugar, and lemon zest in a large bowl until creamy. Mix in the raspberries.

Sprinkle the gelatin over the water in a saucepan. Let stand 1 minute. Stir over low heat until the gelatin has dissolved.

Beat the cream in a medium bowl until stiff. Fold the cream and the gelatin mixture into the raspberry mixture.

Split the cake in three horizontally. Place one layer on a serving plate. Brush with the syrup. Spread with half the raspberry mixture. Top with a second layer and spread with the remaining raspberry mixture. Top with the remaining layer. Brush with the remaining syrup.

Heat the raspberry preserves in a saucepan until liquid. Spread over the cake. Decorate with the raspberries.

Refrigerate for 1 hour before serving.

Italian Sponge Cake
3 large eggs
½ cup (100 g) granulated sugar
⅔ cup (100 g) all-purpose (plain) flour
2 teaspoons baking powder

Filling
1 lb (500 g) raspberries
   (reserve 12 to decorate)
1⅔ cups (250 g) confectioners' (icing)
   sugar
1 cup (250 ml) kirsch
1 cup (250 g) mascarpone
1 tablespoon finely grated lemon zest
1¼ cups (300 ml) heavy (double) cream
2 tablespoons gelatin powder
4 tablespoons cold water
1 (9-inch/23-cm) sponge cake
1 cup (250 g) strained raspberry
   preserves (jam)

Suggested wine: a dry sparkling white
   (Asti Spumante)